Rosalía
de Castro

Galician Songs

Rosalía de Castro

Galician Songs

Translated from Galician by Erín Moure

XUNTA DE GALICIA   Small Stations Press

Small Stations Press
Registered address: 1-A Jose De San Martin Street, 1111 Sofia, Bulgaria
You can order books and contact the publisher at
www.smallstations.com

English translation © Erín Moure, 2013
Design © Yana Levieva, 2013
© Small Stations Press, 2013
© Xunta de Galicia, 2013

First published in Galician as *Cantares gallegos* by Establecimiento tipográfico de
D. J. Compañel, Vigo, in 1863 with a new, corrected and enlarged edition published
by Librería de D. Leocadio López, Madrid, in 1872. This translation follows the
1872 edition, in which four poems (5, 9, 27, 32) have been added, and includes in an
appendix two poems added to the third, posthumous edition published by Librería de
los Sucesores de Hernando, Madrid, in 1909. This makes for a total of 38 poems, one
of which is a response to a poem by Ventura Ruiz Aguilera, which is also included.

The publishers gratefully acknowledge the use of the cover image of Rosalía
de Castro by María Cardarelly supplied by the archive of the Royal Galician
Academy (www.realacademiagalega.org).

ISBN 978-954-384-017-5
Legal deposit C 18-2013

Contents

7 Translator's Introduction: Open That Window,
I Want to See the Sea

19 **GALICIAN SONGS**

21 Dedication

23 Prologue

27 *Sing out, girl*

34 I was born when plants
were born

35 God bless us all, child

40 *Roosters sing the dawn of day*

43 *My sweetliness*

48 *Our Lady of the Barque*

55 'Twas on a Sunday

58 A portly bagpiper

60 The priest once warned me

64 I loved you so much, girl

65 *Bells of Bastabales*

69 I saw you on a clear night

72 *Blessed Saint Anthony*

75 Over there atop

77 *Goodbye, rivers, goodbye, springs*

80 *I clearly saw the owl there*

83 *Little breezes, breezy breezes*

87 Ruddy as the golden sun

91 Roll on, river, roll on, river

93 *Hey, sweet baby boy, hey*

98 *I'm not saying a thing*

105 *But however much he wished*

108 Castilian lady of Castile

111 Sweet light of my eyes

115 Out in the most lovely spot

129 Dear girl, you the most
gorgeous

132 What's up with the boyfriend?

135 *Castilians of Castile*

139 The Galician Bagpipe
(by Ventura Ruiz Aguilera)

142 The Galician Bagpipe
(by Rosalía de Castro)

146 Come on, little girl

151 When moonlight appears

153 If you'd come to see us,
Marica, the other day

155 *How softly it's raining*

163 My dear wondrous Margaret

165 Alborada

170 *I sing out, I sing, I sang*

172 Appendix: Two Poems
Added to the 1909 Edition

180 Glossary

182 Index of Titles/First Lines

183 Index of Titles/First Lines
in Galician

Open That Window, I Want to See the Sea
Abre esa ventana que quiero ver el mar.

Rosalía de Castro

She attends her ear to the smallest of musics: rhythms of words and how they operate in transporting song and conversation onto the page. How line breaks work. Rhyme. How a *copla* or popular ditty might function in poetry on the page: as a break or cut, a 'secession,' as Chus Pato might say. I follow her with my ear, my eye, opening to the textures and rhythms.

Rosalía de Castro works with a delicacy and sure touch that has been the envy of poets for well over a century. The 1872 edition of her *Cantares gallegos* (lent me in photocopy by Jonathan Dunne[1]; the work originally appeared in 1863) is the edition that to my eye most reveals the beauty of the text, its textures and textility, its tensions on the page. In this edition, in so many poems, the *coplas* or verses are delicately separated, allowed to stand on their own as well as exist inside their longer poem sequence. In this way, they appear as popular songs were once sung, for often each listener was also a singer and could raise their voice to add a stanza to embellish or move forward the stanza of the previous one.

Popular ballads, *coplas*, popular songs: in English we might hear them called 'ditties' (ditty, from French, *dite*, a saying, a thing dictated, spoken) or 'doggerel' (verse badly written or expressed). These are terms of derision; high literary culture takes its distance from popular verses, chants, ditties, proverbs and sayings in rhyme. Rosalía de Castro, in *Cantares gallegos*, dares to present a popular tradition as worthy of exploring as contemporary in poetry. Even in her time, that was radical. And Rosalía doesn't merely present readers of her time or of ours with ready-made or recuperated myths or ditties or songs; she listens acutely and then writes her own in a kind of transmission-loop

---

[1] In the public domain, and I discovered it's available for free download as a pdf (not searchable, alas) at http://books.google.com.ec/books?id=phsoAAAA YAAJ. Download it and follow along!

that belies any notion of 'original.' *We* are original, she knows, *because* we copy, we echo, we repurpose texts and so renew them originally. As she does so, Rosalía de Castro honours the orality and transmission not of one, but of a great number of forms, and she does it – most critically – in the language of her own space/time continuum: Galician[2].

This was a cultural secession in its time and still is in ours. Rosalía dares to present her work in Galician, *galego*, a language that, though predominant in medieval times[3], had long since been considered unfit for high culture and was, by Rosalía's time, deemed – by the Galician middle and bourgeois classes and by the Spanish – to be incapable of receiving modernity. Rosalía's *Cantares gallegos* or *Galician Songs*, as a book of poems in Galician, produced a cut or *fenda* in the Galician culture of its day. It is marked as the initial work in the *Rexurdimento* or Revival of Galician-language literature. The book first appeared sometime around 17 May 1863, printed through the offices of Rosalía's husband Manuel Murguía by the Vigo printer Juan Compañel (Rosalía's dedication is dated 17 May 1863). Since the centenary of the book's publication in 1963, 17 May has been commemorated every year as Galician Literature Day, the *Día das letras galegas*.

Why, though, translate Rosalía de Castro today into English? Why is this imperative? The fact that she wrote in Galician, that there was a Galician Revival, that she wrote under the influence of popular culture, all help provide context, but can't be, on their own, reasons for bringing a nineteenth-century Galician

---

[2] Galician and Portuguese share the same medieval root – Galician-Portuguese – and with a bit of effort are still mutually understandable. The northernmost part of old Roman Gallaecia (from the Miño River north) has remained in the state of Spain while the south (to the Douro River) became part of Portugal, where the language flourished, grew and spread to Portuguese colonies. In Galicia, the native language has been much threatened by the almost complete administrative dominance of Castilian Spanish; in Rosalía's time, the language had no official status and people could not learn in their native tongue. Though Galicia is now an Autonomous Community in post-Franco Spain and Galician and Castilian are both co-official, Galician still struggles not to lose ground today. There is currently, however, a huge literature in Galician, which was not the case in Rosalía's time.

[3] It was the one language used for lyric poetry across the Iberian peninsula.

poet into English-speaking language and literary cultures in 2013. The history of another literature is interesting, but does not mean a work has a vital place in our cultures, that it is and can be our contemporary. Yet Rosalía de Castro does have a vital place with us and is my contemporary and yours.

In *Malaise dans l'esthétique* (*A Malaise in Aesthetics*), French philosopher Jacques Rancière writes of the relation between art and politics in a way that I find useful for understanding the common denigration of popular culture and Rosalía's revolutionary use of it and how and why her work is useful to us today. 'Always,' says Rancière, 'the refusal to consider certain categories of people as political beings starts with the refusal to understand the sounds coming from their mouths as discourse.'[4] He continues, 'Politics exists when those who "don't have" time [artisans, workers] take this time required to position themselves as inhabitants of common space and to demonstrate that their mouths indeed emit speech that enunciates the commons and not just singular voices that signal pain. This distribution and redistribution of places and identities, this division and redivision of spaces and times, of the visible and the invisible, of noise and speech, constitutes what I call the distribution of the sensible.'[5]

Rosalía creates, in her works in poetry, that Rancièrean space for others to be heard, though it is not – yet – the people who assume their own voices, who take the time to demonstrate that their mouths emit discourse. She speaks for them, through them, to demonstrate this. As such, in her poems, the villagers of Galicia do not occupy the space of the commons in Rancière's sense. Yet when we hear that prior voice that signals pain, we

---

[4] 'De tout temps, le refus de considérer certaines catégories de personnes comme des êtres politiques est passé par le refus d'entendre les sons sortant de leur bouche comme du discours.' (38)

[5] 'La politique advient lorsque eux qui "n'ont pas" le temps prennent ce temps nécessaire pour se poser en habitants d'un espace commun et pour démontrer que leur bouche émet bien une parole qui énonce du commun et non seulement une voix qui signale la douleur. Cette distribution et cette redistribution des places et des identités, ce découpage et ce redécoupage des espaces et des temps, du visible et de l'invisible, du bruit et de la parole constituent ce que j'appelle le partage du sensible.' (38)

hear it not simply as individual; across the voices in the book, it is a crescendo. And the voice is not just one of pain, but is also the voice of praise. In the Rancièrean sense, politics had not arrived for the Galicians in her time and arguably – given the constant struggles over the right to education in Galician and the right to speak Galician in all spheres of life – has not arrived fully today for Galician speakers in Galicia. Even so, Rosalía's voice in these poems from the nineteenth century and now from our century – *is* a voice in discourse and one that understands the sounds coming from the mouths of the villagers as discourse. In this alone, Rosalía de Castro is exemplary, not just in Galician, but in the Western European literature of her day. Most European poetry of the Romantic age does not have this relationship with ordinary people, does not consider their voices as voices in discourse. In a sense, Rosalía's could be considered a feminist move, one that had to await the feminist arguments that infuse late twentieth-century literature to assume its place. This understanding and capacity for discourse in the helix of her poems, and the way she borrows from and harnesses older popular forms without being constrained by them, make her, I believe, our contemporary.

Her work captures rhythms of speech and folk stories with a delicacy and cadence. She used and altered many forms and shapes of folk verse. In her lines, Rosalía could deftly resonate and articulate the roundabout nature of the laments of ordinary people, who complain without complaining (for there's no use in complaining), then go on, winking, leaving you to figure out the punch-line. Rosalía's voice respects those she writes of and acknowledges their agency; Rosalía does not just write 'about,' but alongside them, with them. She takes up the metres of popular songs and stories, of the *cantar*, a chanted and rhyming tale, and invents and inverts rhythms as well. She invents folk sayings that echo, but do not repeat, real sayings. In their textures and complexities, their varied ways of revealing their content and object, her poems glint, echo, coil, uncoil, move, refract.

In translating her, Rosalía's rhythms evoked in me the rhythms of the classic Western songs that I heard as a child and learned on the piano: 'Goodbye Old Paint,' 'Whoopee Ti Yi Yo,' 'Streets of Laredo,' 'Bury Me Not On the Lone Prairie.' I realized that, in the nineteenth century of Atlantic Galicia, Rosalía de Castro was writing what might be seen as kin to our Western music as in the work of American greats such as Woody Guthrie, Joan Baez, Emmylou Harris, Linda Ronstadt, who took up old songs, made them new and made new songs in the same vein. Rosalía's work, like the best of that genre, was wise, never transmitting clichés about people or religion, about marriage, family, emigration, revolt. She opened and altered the clichés, redirecting time, deploying a poetic 'helix,' as American poet Christian Hawkey would say. Her poems are coiled springs.

Above all, and in a way more powerful than that of the plaintive Western music of my childhood, Rosalía de Castro wrote about women, about women's lives and sexuality, about poor people, about labour abuse and lack of access to education, with a depth of understanding of the economics of human lives that no other writer, woman or man, displayed at that time, not in Spanish and not in English either, as far as I know. Rosalía, as she is universally known, wrote without didacticism. She pulled on all the strengths of popular culture to create occasions for realism, for the glint of ambivalence that keeps us alive, for learning, for double meanings, for social criticism, and to create social space, a commons. Hers is a lyricism that allows the lyric address – of one human voice to another human ear – to ring out in space and time. It is the voice of a Galician Spring, murmured, an *Occupy Galicia* against the forces that did and would treat it badly. She put herself on the line for her people and her language.

The dilemmas of the people who inhabit her poems are eternal; curiously, they are still our dilemmas today. The economy still invades and constructs our bodies in ways that Foucault, Agamben, Negri and Hardt, Žižek and others have articulated in political philosophy. Rosalía writes out of her own transgressed woman's body and writes poems, not political philosophy. She writes from the plenitude of a woman's body that she never occults and is frank and open about women's desire and about how it is met in the world by men, with love at times, but also with cruel violence. Nor is the economy of women's lives missing from the poems – not only men have difficulty making a living. In the poems, Rosalía makes visible the ways that women were forced (and still are at times) to take up with a man to ensure a viable economic life and makes visible the sad and contradictory attraction to men who appear to offer good prospects. This visibility of economic difficulty and worry can lie in the smallest of hints, such as a place-name: when the young girls flirt with the young guys from Cadiz in poem 32, for example, the place-name refers to the Andalusian port far south of Galicia. Cadiz was one of the peninsular ports where emigrants who had succeeded (or who pretended to have succeeded) in America returned to Spain and thence to Galicia, but was also – and Rosalía is adept at hinting at falseness – a catchword for masculine pretence to grandeur. It could be that the young guys from Cadiz are not only not from there, but aren't successes at all. Then, in poem 25, the poor man Vidal's inheritance also comes from 'beyond Cadiz,' which is to say from America.

In articulating sexuality and its consequences, Rosalía is playful; she picks up the rhythms and caginess of folk stories, of the tongue-in-cheek or winking way that stories are told in order not to step outside the boundaries of public acceptance. In poem 13, for example, the narrating woman makes a plea to Saint Anthony – as everyone knew, the saint in charge of finding lost things and thus also a matchmaker – for a man, because she wants a roll in the hay, oh yes, but not with just any bloke or bounder who comes to hang around the house of a single woman. This woman, moreover, has a 'little brother,' by which we can read a baby, and one that can only be her own, the reader surmises, the result of a roll in the hay with one of those men perhaps. It could be that the man she seeks is – since she seeks him of Saint Anthony – the 'lost' (read 'absconded') father of the child. Or perhaps he is any man, for the woman wants a man in the house for her own safety, so she can safely express her sexuality, her sexual hunger. For that, it is good to have a man around, as that 'solves the problem,' as the poem says!

In poem 24 we read a letter from a particular kind of forced emigrant in a country formed by emigration: the army conscript. The poem is traversed by issues of the difficulty of obtaining education if you are poor and by the facts of emigration and conscription, of colonization (for the conscripts of Galicia served in the armies of their ruler, Spain), and by the tenuousness of written expression, the need for a reader at the other end of the helix for the helix to bear meaning. The poem is in the voice of a conscript writing plaintively to the lover left behind in Galicia, who had promised to learn how to read in his absence, so she could read his letters. He writes to her, hoping. And we know (for we are the only readers) that she hasn't learned to read yet at all; this voice and poem are ours alone and never reach the lover. The poem is a condemnation of the social and economic conditions of ordinary people, of colonization and armed force. Yet the writer feels valued in the handsomeness of his uniform! His voice is intact.

In poem 30 I most hear the echoes of something close to call and response; the relationship of the stanzas here is different from in other poems, not quite linear, but contrapuntal. Separate the stanzas with your eye and you'll hear the music of several voices in the room, each trying to match and trump the other with a quatrain of their own. It reminds me of Cuban music, of American jazz, of old sea shanties, of Breton music, in the way the various voices give the poem volume and movement that a linear form would not have. Each poem of Rosalía's is as rich in its provocations and I could go on marvelling at what she achieves. These are just three examples.

Galician Songs forms a unified material whole. The original had 36 poems, 35 numbered and one near the middle not numbered which was, rather, a response to the poem of a Spanish poet concerning the Galician national musical instrument, the

Galician bagpipe or *gaita*, a poem also included. The first and last numbered poems of the book act as prologue and epilogue, book-ending the volume with the fact of a woman raising her voice in song, giving that *gaita* in the middle a squeeze. At one end, in poem 1, a voice incites the young woman to sing; it quickly turns out that it is the young woman speaking, citing the request made of her. She continues to state her reasons for singing before breaking into the song that is the poems that follow. By the end of the poem, we know it is not one person, but a people and language that have called her to sing. At the other end of the book, in poem 36, the woman has sung and excuses her lack of grace. In short, the book is structured so that the nation and its instrument are held in the embrace of this woman's voice.

The first and last poems, along with others in the collection, have been identified by critics as bearing the voice of the author expressing her own feelings rather than creating a voice. Yet even in these poems, the lyric 'I' is not always her 'I,' but is an 'I' played in an open key. It is a folding, in which Rosalía iterates her own belonging to the group of whom she sings. Rosalía rejects those who find the customs and lives of ordinary people to be unworthy of dignity and paints herself as ordinary too. Yet the poems can't simply be defined as rural, patriotic songs, as explorations in Galician of the concept of identity and home, as works on the condition of women and men and the customs of love, which were also customs linked to the economy, to the mill and emigration, to the church with its feasts and processions. They are complex rhythmic and sound gestures, movements which, in their material condition as language, speak to us even when translated, as users of our own language, English, today.

In translating Rosalía, I learned many things about Galician. I made extensive and constant use of the online, amalgamated Galician 'Dictionary of Dictionaries' (http://sli.uvigo.es/ddd/index.html) maintained by the University of Vigo, to which I owe thanks, particularly to professor Xavier Gómez Guinovart, who answered my weekend pleas when the server was down;

this book could not have existed in English had I not a way to look up the meanings of older words and words not in contemporary dictionaries. I have to thank, as well, poet Chus Pato, whose support of my endeavours and re-explanations of certain parts of poems helped me to be sure I was understanding as a Galician would understand. To Jonathan Dunne, Galician translator and publisher of Galician works in English, I owe the funding and encouragement to translate this book. And I thank professor and critic Arturo Casas for his very astute and useful feedback on this introduction.

It will come as no surprise that I noticed a lot about English as well, as I translated. It surprised me how French words have come into our dictionary, but not Galician or Spanish, even when the word in question started in Galician or Spanish! In English, I could entitle poem 35 ('Alborada' in Galician) 'Aubade,' using the French word which exists in English as well, but when I looked it up, my dictionary reported that the French word comes from the Provençal *auba*, dawn, and perhaps from the Spanish *albada*, which comes from *alborada* (meanwhile my French dictionary, less willing to admit a Provençal ancestry for the word, claimed only that it came from Latin). Back almost where I started, I decided that 'Aubade' doesn't transmit the flavour of this amazing poem of Rosalía's, where she breaks every tradition of her contemporary poetry to imitate the sound of a musical piece, anticipating John Cage as she does so. In English, finally, I titled it 'Alborada.' If you search for 'alborada galega' or 'alborada gallega' on YouTube, you'll be able to listen to the music whose sounds awakened the words of poetry in Rosalía. Electrifying! You can also find music of the *muiñeira* on YouTube, for in poems 5 and 17 I left the word '*muiñeira*,' unable to pull it out and just put 'mill reel.'

I do have one regret. Perhaps I'll solve it in a future translation. It is that Rosalía's spelling and materiality are impossible to replicate. If I invented a spelling and sounding in English to match hers, I'd only sound archaic or odd, and Rosalía was neither. In Rosalía's case, her Galician is vigorously modern and her pen sure, but the material texture of her written language is affected by colonization, land politics, the education system, the entire gamut of events and oppressions and infiltrations that pressured the Galician language, which didn't even have a written grammar in Rosalía's time. Rosalía is inventive and changes words, practically invents them at times, moving her mouth and translating the smallest quiver of a muscle into alphabetic script. I think of 'curbadeira' in poem 33, a word that I couldn't find anywhere, but could best guess to be akin to 'curvatura.' In the end, I wasn't wrong and it *was* in my own Xerais Gran Dicionario as 'curvadeira,' a now non-normative word meaning 'undulation,' 'curve.' Many Galician words are like this one, reformed and remade by Rosalía, echoing local usages and musics to which we now have no direct access. I had to move the word in my mouth, speak from the Galician part of the body, listen to the sound of the word, hear it in the air, before I could figure out what it was (and then look it up in the dictionaries!). Rosalía certainly does have this effect. When I read her in the original, I start to feel *her* pronunciation in my mouth and inhabit the words with her mouth… a strange and lovely feeling.

Just who was this woman, this poet whose work started a resurgence in Galician-language culture? She was a woman born in modest but educated circumstances, not uncommon in nineteenth-century Galicia. Her father was a Catholic priest[6] and her mother unmarried (well, marrying a Catholic priest is impossible), a *fidalga* by class, meaning someone of landowning heritage, though her family was, by this time, of modest economic means. Given the official shame of her progenitors' relationship, Rosalía was baptized as being of unknown parents. She avoided the orphanage by being carried

---

[6] Because Galician landholdings were tiny, young adults left the family land to the first-born and went to make their living elsewhere. The oldest who stayed was responsible for the parents and for unmarried children who remained. Often second sons went into the military or into the priesthood in order to reduce the burden on the first-born. These priests by profession rather than vocation often enough had children. Of course this was officially forbidden and so these children were often brought up by relatives and knew their father as an 'uncle.' In this way, the family found new, albeit truncated, forms and managed to stay together, as in Rosalía's case.

away by her godmother, a servant in her mother's family, who had brought her for baptism. She was first raised by her father's sister in Castro de Ortoño, where she would have become aware of the language, customs and poverty of Galician villagers. At some point after she turned eight, enough time had elapsed since her birth for decency's sake and she lived with her mother, first in Padrón, then in Santiago de Compostela. Grown up and educated as were other women of her class, she moved around a lot, following her husband, the intellectual and active Galicianist Manuel Murguía, where his career took him. Her last years were spent in Galicia and she died there, in Padrón, where she had first lived with her mother. The full circle of a life.

Padrón was once on the sea, they say. In myth as recorded in the Codex Calixtinus, the body of the Christian apostle James arrived by sea on a stone boat from Jerusalem to touch shore at Iria Flavia, just one kilometre from Padrón. Now, though the pilgrimage to the apostle's tomb in Santiago de Compostela is legendary, the small, nearby harbour is long silted up; it takes a special power to see the sea from Padrón. The desire to see the sea is, I think, a desire for infinity, for the wash of the uncountable molecules that suspend light and, deeper down, darkness in and of us. At noon on 15 July 1885, when Rosalía de Castro was dying of cancer in her house in Padrón, folklore has it that her last words were '*Abre esa ventana que quiero ver el mar*' – 'Open that window, I want to see the sea.'

Galician Songs is also a window onto a sea. And is ours, our sea, our window. As Galician writer Manuel Rivas said in April 2012 on Irish television in Galway, 'Books are emigrants and belong in the place where they arrive. When a reader opens a book, the book also opens the reader.' In opening this book, we can receive Rosalía de Castro as contemporary to us in English and answer her challenges with future work of our own.

Erín Moure

REFERENCES

Lomax, John. *Cowboy Songs and Other Frontier Ballads*. New York: Sturgis & Walton, 1911. http://digitalcommons.unl.edu/cgi/viewcontent.cgi?article=1011&context=englishunsllc

Pato, Chus. *Secesión*. Vigo: Galaxia, 2009.

Pato, Chus. *Secession*. Trans. Erín Moure. Montreal: Zat-So Productions, 2012. Limited edition for Rotterdam Festival.

Rancière, Jacques. *Malaise dans l'esthétique*, Paris: Galilée, 2004. Quotes in this introduction were translated into English by Erín Moure.

Rivas, Manuel. RTÉ International (Raidió Teilifís Éireann), accessed 8 May 2012, in a report on the Galway literary festival Cúirt. Trans. Jonathan Dunne, altered slightly. http://www.rte.ie/player/#v=1147948

Galician Songs

Madam, As you are a woman and novelist whose works I have found deeply sympathetic, I dedicate this small book to you. It will serve to demonstrate to you, author of *La Gaviota* and *Clemencia*, my great appreciation for, among other things, the way you avoided, in your pages that touch on Galicia, the vulgar ideas with which some try to taint my country.

Rosalía de Castro de Murguía
Santiago de Compostela, 17 May 1863

It is a bold move for a poor innocent such as myself to publish a book whose pages should brim with the sun, harmony and naturality that – with deep tenderness and the incessant murmur of sweet affectionate words – infuse our popular verse with such beauty. Galician poetry – with its music and vagaries, laments, sighs and shy smiles, and the way it murmurs like mysterious forest winds or shines like a sunbeam serenely cast on the waters of a full river racing under flowering willow branches – should be sung by a sublime and Christian spirit, if I can say that, in inspiration as fecund as the greenery that beautifies our privileged land. Above all, it should be sung with delicate and penetrating feeling, so as to reveal the primal beauty – fugitive rays of beauty – that glows in each tradition and thought of this people whom many have called stupid and have judged to be insensitive, foreign to the divine art of poetry. Yet no one, even I, has the qualities needed to carry out such difficult work; neither is anyone else prompted to sing the beauties of our land in our suave and sweet Galician tongue, that some insist is a barbaric dialect; they don't recognize how sweet and harmonious it is compared to other languages. My own efforts are weak and unlettered, apart from what I've learned from our poor villagers, and are guided only by the songs, cherished words and remembered sayings that have resonated in my ears since I was in the cradle and that I hold in my heart as my heritage. So I dared to write these songs, wanting to make known the ancestral and primitive freshness of our poetic tradition, and show that our sonorous and sweet dialect is as good as any other.

My efforts, it is true, did not live up to my dreams, and when I think how much better a great poet could have done, my insufficiency pains me even more. The *Book of Songs* by Antonio Trueba, that inspired me and propelled me to create this work, lies remorsefully in my thoughts, and I almost cry when I think how Galicia would be raised to its rightful position if a poet like Antonio had been destined to make known its beauties and customs. But my unhappy country, unlucky in this too, has to content itself with my few cold and insipid pages that would hardly deign to arrive at the gates of Parnassus if it weren't for the noble feelings that created them. May these feelings serve to excuse me to those who justly criticize my faults, for I think that those who struggle to erase the errors that stain and unjustly offend their country are entitled to some indulgence!

Chants, tears, laments, sighs, sunsets, processions, landscapes, pastures, pine groves, longings, shores, customs, all that by its form and coloration merits being sung in poetry, all that has had an echo, a voice, a rumour however soft, that comes to move me, all this I have dared to sing in this humble book, so as to say, once and for all, even if clumsily, to those who despise us without reason or knowledge, that our land is worthy of praise, and our language is not the one they bastardize and mangle in more educated provinces with derisory laughter that only (as harsh as it might seem to say) demonstrates the crass ignorance and most unforgivable injustice that one province can inflict on its neighbour, however poor it may be. What is the saddest in this matter is the falsehood with which the children of Galicia, and Galicia itself, are portrayed in other places, and how it is judged to be the most despicable and ugly part of Spain, when it is really the most beautiful and worthy of exaltation.

I do not wish to wound anyone's feelings by saying this, although, to be frank, there is nothing more forgivable than this little blast from one who has endured the most wounds of all. But I have travelled many times across the solitude of desert-like Castile; I have passed through fertile Extremadura and expansive La Mancha, where the leaden sun falls and illuminates monotonous fields in which a dry straw colour lends the landscape a tired tone that overwhelms and saddens the spirit, without a blade of grass to distract the gaze that is lost in cloudless sky as unchanging and tiring as the land below it; I have visited the celebrated region of Alicante, where rows of dark green olive trees appear to weep to find themselves so alone; and I have seen the famed gardens of Murcia, so renowned and praised, which, tired and monotonous like the rest of that country, display their vegetation like painted landscapes with trees placed in symmetrical rows for children to play among. Given all this, I can't but feel indignant when the children of provinces fully favoured by God – though not in the beauty of their fields – poke fun at Galicia whose climate and grace compete with the most enchanting countries in the world, this Galicia where all is spontaneous in nature and where the human hand cedes its place to the hand of God.

Lakes, cascades, torrents, flowering plains, valleys, mountains, skies as blue and serene as those of Italy, melancholy and cloudy but still beautiful horizons that rival those of lauded Switzerland, peaceful and serene shores, tempestuous capes whose immense and deafening fury elicits terror and admiration, immense seas: what more can I say? There's no pen able to enumerate the whole of so much wonder. The earth is covered year-round with grasses and flowers, the mountains full of pines, oaks and willows, soft winds that blow, crystalline springs and torrents that burble summer and winter through cheerful fields in deep and sombre catapults. Galicia is a garden exhaling pure aromas, freshness and poetry! Despite this, we have to put up with the fatuousness of ignoramuses, the mean bias that exists against our land, so that even those who have come to contemplate all this loveliness (never mind those who joke at our expense without ever having been here, and they are legion), even those who have entered Galicia and enjoyed the delights it offers, have dared to call Galicia... a squalid stable!!!! And those people perhaps came from lands so scorched by sun that even small birds flee them! How on earth are we to respond to this? It's worth noting that such fatuousness sounds like the French who prate about their eternal victories over the Spanish. To hear them tell it, Spain never ever triumphed; on the contrary, it was always vanquished, fallen, humiliated. The saddest part of this is that it's a bare-faced lie, just as it is when dry Castile, desert-like La Mancha and all the other provinces of Spain, none with landscapes of true beauty comparable to ours, call Galicia the most unpleasant corner of the earth. If we remember that 'what goes round comes round,' it is no surprise that Spain comes to suffer the constant insults from a neighbouring nation in the same unfair way that it, even more blameworthy, treats a humiliated province which it only brings to mind to humiliate even more. I too feel hurt by the injustices heaped upon Spain by the French, but sometimes I almost thank them, for they provide me a way to palpably demonstrate the injustice that Spain in its turn commits against Galicia.

This was the main motivation that impelled me to publish this book which all too often, I know, pleads for everyone's indulgence. In the absence of any kind of grammar or rules, the reader will often notice spelling errors and phrases that will ring badly in the ears of a purist. At least, and to partly excuse these defects, I took the greatest of care to reproduce the real spirit of our people, and I think I somehow succeeded, even if in a weak and meagre way. Heaven knows that someone more worthy than I am could have better described the veritable colours and enchanting images found here even in the most hidden and forgotten corners, so that, at least in renown if not in concrete benefits, our unlucky Galicia could gain the respect and be seen with the admiration it deserves!

1

Sing out, girl,
I'll give you hot chestnuts;
Sing out, girl,
I'll give more than a few.

I

'Sing out,
Gleeful sweet girl,
Sing out,
For such heartaches I bear.

Sing out, girl,
At the lip of the fountain,
Sing, I will give you
Dumplings in broth.

Sing out, girl,
In soothing rhythms,
I'll give you a pancake
From the stone of the hearth.

Polenta with milk
I will also provide you,
Bread sopped in wine,
Honeyed egg toast.

Roasted potatoes
Salted and vinegared,
That taste of walnuts,
So savoury they are!

What a party, my girl,
We'll have if you'll sing!…
Carousing outdoors,
Carousing inside.

Sing if you will,
My impish young girl,
Sing if you will,
I'll give you a pinafore.

Sing if you will,
In my own tongue, Galician,
I'll give you a pinafore,
I'll give you petticoats.

To the sound of sweet bagpipes,
To the sound of tambourine,
I ask you to sing to me,
Oh dark lovely girl.

To the sound of the bagpipe,
To the sound of the drum,
I ask you to sing to me,
Sweet girl, in God's name.'

II

That's what they asked me
At the shore of the sea,
At the foot of the wavelets
That lap and ebb.

That's what they asked me
On the bank of the stream
That tips through the grasses
Of the flowering field.

The crickets were trilling,
The roosters, they crowed,
The wind in the leaves
Passed rustling by.

The pastures were glowing,
The springs welled up
Between grass and grapevine,
Fig tree and oak.

The bagpipes were playing,
To the beat of tambourines,
The young men were dancing
With girls so demure.

How white their starched bonnets!
Their shawls so fringed!…
What coverlets of scarlet!
What ribbons! What lace!

What lovely aprons,
What green petticoats…
What well-cut waistcoats
Of scarlet hues!

Such lively colours
Make the sight blur:
On seeing them so varied,
The sun tarries too.

To see them bustling
On mountains and plains,
You'd think they were roses
Gallant and fresh.

III

No place prettier than this
Is there on the earth,
Than this one I see,
Than this one given me.

A place prettier than this
In the world you'll not find,
Than that of Galicia,
Charming Galicia!

Galicia in flower,
There's no place like this,
Covered in flowers,
Covered in mists.

In mists that the sea
Casts up with its pearls,
In flowers that flourish
At the foot of springs.

In valleys so deep,
So green, so fresh,
That heartsickness calms
When they come into sight.

May the wee angels there
Keep sleeping so still,
In the form of doves,
In the form of mists.

IV

To sing you, Galicia,
Your own sweet songs.
That's what they asked me
On the shore of the sea.

To sing you, Galicia,
In Galician our tongue,
Solace from misfortune,
Release from despair.

Sweet, smooth,
Deeply felt, melancholy,
It charms and laughs,
Moves and weeps.

With Galician, there's no other
Language as sweet, to sing
Bitter longings,
Sighs of love.

Mysteries of afternoon,
Murmurings of night,
To sing you, Galicia,
At the lip of your springs.

I'm asked this and this only
They insist of me:
That I sing and I sing
In the language I speak.

Since they ask me,
Since they urge me to sing…
I'm singing, sweet girls,
Get ready, I'll begin.

With sweet joy,
In soothing rhythms,
At the foot of wavelets,
That lap and ebb.

May God allow
These songs that I sing
To bring you respite
From your grief.

Some friendly consolation,
Some quiet contentment,
Full of fortune
And fulfilled desires.

By night, by day,
At dawn, at sunset,
You'll hear me singing
Across peaks and plains.

Whoever calls to me,
Whoever asks me
To sing, I'll sing to them
All night and day.

To bring contentment,
To give consolation,
Turning to smiles
All woe and tears.

Seek me out, girls,
Old crones, young gallants,
Seek me amid oak trees
And between stalks of corn.

In the portals of the rich,
At the doors of the poor,
For these songs I sing
Are intended for all.

For all, who pray
To the Virgin for help,
So that she'll console you
In your suffering.

In your torments,
In your griefs.
Okay, time to sing…
On with it, by God!

2

I was born when plants were born,
In the month of flowers I was born,
In a gentle dawn,
In a dawn of April.
That's why they called me Rosie,
The rose that smiles sadly,
With thorns for all comers,
But no thorns for you.
From the time I loved you, ingrate,
It was all over for me,
You were all mine,
My glory and life.
So why are you grumbling, Mauro?
Why are you grumbling, say it,
When you know that I'd die
To see you happy?
Cruel slave, you entrapped me
With your slanderous words,
With your crazy demands;
Till I don't know what you want of me,
I told you what I could give,
Enrapt I was for you.
My heart I send to you
With a key to open it,
I can give you nothing greater,
Nor you ask more of me.

3

'God bless us all, child,
Girl, may God bless you,
For he made you so graceful,
For he made you so lovely,
And though many lands I've wandered,
Though I've passed through many towns,
I've never seen a girl like you
So shapely and pretty too.
I praise the one who bore you!
Amen, I laud the one who raised you!'

'May God be with you, Granny,
May the Virgin keep you safe,
For you speak so well,
Well-spoken and persuasive.'

'Dear girl, in speaking well
There's nothing to lose:
Those that sing best
Can fly with songbirds;
The chick who doesn't chirp
Dies choked in the straw.'

'But if you were a wee chick,
I tell you, Granny dear,
You'd never die of choking,
When you chirp you chirp so well.'

'Oh, that's never been my fate,
My daughter, my girl!
For I was born an orphan,
With no love in the world;

From door to door begging
I've had to spend my days.
And oh, my life is passing,
Oh this pilgrim life of mine,
I seek as I wander begging
My daily bread each day,
Always in strangers' doorways,
Always in strange towns,
I have to pull myself onward
So I don't die in desperation,
Fallen by a wall
And forgotten by all,
The chirp of little birdies,
The clamour of doves,
The smooth tongue that's essential,
The quiet humility it takes.'

'You are wise, dear Granny,
Your knowledge is huge!
We'd have to wander the world
To be as wise as you are!
Even though it's hard work
Afar in distant towns,
Yet what things are learned!
Yet what things are seen!'

'You'd see so many valleys
You'd get lost for sure:
What the sun's gaze procures
Is left later in the dark!'

''Tis truth you tell, dear Granny,
But your eyes are so clear,
As if they'd been lent you
By the glorious Saint Lucy.'

'I am devoted to her,
She is my blessed saint!
But clear eyes aren't always
A proof of clear sight.
Many eyes glance like water
That races between cold peaks
Gurgling as it passes,
Serene, serene,
Where darkness once goaded,
Where gloom once lived,
In the dark gloom of sins
Hidden furthest away.'

'If you're talking of sin,
It's bread that grows
Wherever you look;
It's cultivated all over;
Yet some grains are poisoned,
Others dark as boiled blood,
Others, black as night,
Grow alongside lurking slatterns,
Who part their gold and silk
Wrapped up in envy,
Nourished by lust,
Flattered by greed.'

'Leave well enough alone,
Let it be, my girl,
Don't long to wander,
Nor see distant towns,
For the world betrays
Those who don its finery
And in towns you'd get into
Things you'd never do here,
For though rotten grain
Sprouts up everywhere,

In some places it hardly grows,
In others it shoots up high.'

'You talk like a lawyer
And anyone would think
That you'd learned in books
Such highfalutin words,
All so well spoken,
All so understanding.
You've put the fear into me
So I'd not leave from here
Without the Holy Bible
And medallions all blessed
In the pocket of my waistcoat,
Along with an amulet of jet,
To protect me from witches
And from slatterns who lurk.'

'May they save you from yourself,
Ask God this, young lady fine,
We ourselves are the slatterns
Who'd do us the worst.
But look, night is coming
With its mantle of stars,
The cows have been herded
From the paddock where they graze,
Far off the bells are ringing,
They peel the Angelus,
Every rabbit to its burrow
Nimbly, nimbly heads,
For night's a foul companion
If a companion is required.
But oh, I have no burrow
Or spot to lie me down,
Nor roof to protect me
From cold night winds!

What a life the poor lead, child!
What a life, a bitter lot!
But Our Saviour was poor
And this brings us relief.'

'Amen, old Granny, amen,
But by the holy souls I swear
Today you'll sleep in a bed
Made of wheaten straw,
Beside a hearth to warm you
With cinders aglow,
And you'll eat a hot broth
With potatoes and greens.'

'Blessed be God, blessed,
Blessed the Virgin be
Who brings me such goodness
With a compassionate hand!
May the Saviour grant you fortune
And a life of many years;
May your roof-tiles turn to gold
And flagstones to fine silver
And may every grain become
A diamond for you each day!
And now, my girl,
For it's time you had fun
Dancing with your girlfriends
Who gossip in the kitchen,
I'll have to tell you tales,
I'll have to sing you songs,
I'll clap shells to keep time,
My sweet kerchiefed girl!'

4

'Roosters sing the dawn of day,
Get up, my darling, and go.'
'Why do I have to go, sweetie,
Why do I have to go and leave you?'

'Those black eyes of yours,
Like two glowing rosary beads,
Down to our entwined hands
Let ardent tears fall.
Why do I have to go if I love you?
Why do I have to go and leave you
When your tongue sends me away
And your heart beckons me?
In a corner of your bed
Lovingly you sheltered me;
With your gentle warmth
You warmed my cold feet;
And from here we gazed together
Between the green branches
At how the moon was racing
Over the pine groves.
How can you wish I leave you,
How can I tear myself away,
When you've been sweeter than honey
And more delicate than flowers?'

'Charmer, you sweet charmer,
You who charmed me into love,
Go from me now, charmer,
Before the sun comes up.'

'Hush, sleep on, my dearest,
Between the wavelets of the sea,
Sleep so you may caress me
And call me your own love,
Only at your side, dear girl,
Can I rest content.'

'The songbirds already sing,
Get up, my love, it's late.'

'Let them sing, Marica,
Marica, let them sing…
Though you wish that I would go,
I wish madly to remain.'

'With me, my sweetest lover,
Half the night you've spent.'

'But while you were asleep,
I was happy in watching you,
As you smiled in your dreams
You looked just like an angel,
But I'd never wait for an angel
With such purity.'

'I do love you, my sweetheart,
Like a saint on the altar high,
But flee… for the golden sun
Peeks over the mountain crest.'

'I'll go, but kiss me quickly
Before I part from you,
For oh, those lips of roses,
I still wonder how they taste.'

'I'll give you a kiss so loving,
But I'll have to go confess,
For it was very shameful
To have sinned so greatly.'

'So go confess, Marica,
But when it's married we are,
You'll no longer have need, sweetie,
Of confessors or friars.
Farewell, sweet rosy cheeks!'

'May God protect you, love!'

5

My sweetliness,
My saintly familiar,
My sweet face
A pumpkin so cute.
  I'll lend you
My pendants,
I'll lend you
My necklace;
    I'll lend it you,
Sweet face,
If you teach me
To step-dance.

  'Little seamstress,
Little flatterer,
Hoe in the field,
Flail in the threshing yard,
    Wash up in the river,
Go spread gorse
Branches to dry
In the pines.
    That's how a
Hard-working girl
Will learn
To step-dance.'

  'My sweetliness,
The one who advises me
To do all that
Doesn't love me!

Hands of a lady,
Hands so patrician,
All seamstresses
Have them;
  Mouth of a queen,
Body of a damsel,
Silk is what suits them,
They flee the mud.'

  'Ho, little flirty,
Your head's in the clouds!
Silk for those who lie down
Out in the rye!
  To flee from the mud
When you were born in it!
May God forgive you,
Poor Manuela.
  Honourable mud
Never smirched anything
And no silk will clean
Honour that's sullied.'

  'My saintly familiar,
You're taking me wrong,
Saying such things
That are so hurtful.
  I was only talking
Of the *muiñeiras*,
Those dance spins and
Sashays,
  Of those footsteps
That they dance now,
Forward and back,
From back to fore.'

'Sweet little seamstress
Of the oaken grove,
Take up a needle,
Take up a thimble,
    Sew up the holes
In that blouse of yours,
God doesn't want us
To go around ragged.
    Sew, little woman,
Every rip, every tear,
And you'll not think
Of dance steps.'

    'My saintly familiar,
My sweetliness,
I have no needle,
I have no thread,
    Nor thimble have I,
For down at the fair
A dandy filched them
Out of my wallet,
    Saying, "What the absent-
Minded lose
The well-heeled
Can use."'

    'Sweet little seamstress
Who listens to dandies!
Soul of copper,
Necklace of silver,
    Youth scuppered,
Old age in tears…
Get going, girlie,
And mind the cows.

Mind the herbs
In your kitchen garden,
You'll have a needle,
You'll have a thimble.'

'Oh, skip the herbs,
What I'd rather do
Is go with the girls
To the fair.
　　And there so sprightly
Spin every dance!
Eyes lowered,
Legs flying.
　　Fleet of foot,
Body held tall,
But my sweetliness…
You don't make it easy!
　　Cut out your
Preaching,
Help me be
A dancer.
　　You from the hill,
Come on the run;
You can dance high step
And having learned
　　You go while I pine
Along the crags…
Look what I'm asking
In an ocean of tears.'

'Oh young woman!
Oh, what tears!
Oh, because you want
To be a dancer!

When you're asleep
In the graveyard,
Your enemies
Will scare you
      Dancing on top
Of silent grasses,
To the sound of the black
Bagpipe of Judas.
      And that dainty body
That once
Danced so much
At all the fairs
      To the sound of winds
At their most vicious
She'll roll then
With the damned.
      Sweet little seamstress,
I'm not the one, no,
Who'll teach you
Such bad ways.'

      'Oh, what a saintliness!
Oh, what a fat saint!
Eyes of a witch,
Face of a monkey,
      I won't lend you
My pendants,
Won't let you wear
My necklace,
      Because you don't want to,
Because you won't think of
Teaching me
To step-dance.'

6

Our Lady of the Barque
Has a canopy of stone:
You could have one of gold,
My Lady, just say the word.

I

Oh, what crowds... what crowds
From farm fields and plains!
So many at low tide
Arrive walking on the shore!
What launches festooned
In garlands for the party!
What boats so handsome,
With beautiful sails!
They come packed tight
With folk from afar
And with beautiful lasses,
Cure of all heartaches.
All those scarlet shawls!
All those yellow ribbons!
All those ironed bonnets
That shine from a distance,
As if they're pure snow,
As if they're spring flowers!
So dashing are the men!
So fair all the girls!
And the men strapping as
Pines that glow on the mountains
And the women sweet buds
That morning dew freshens.

The girls from Muros, so dainty
You'd think they'd break,
With those virginal faces,
With those almond eyes,
With those long locks
Tied up in long braids,
With their rosy cheeks
As if brushed by dawn,
For they are so suave
Like dawn's first peek;
Descendants of the airy
Daughters of pagan Greece,
Dressed in black skirts,
They're so slim and light,
Black petticoats and aprons,
Shoes and silk stockings,
Black vests of satin,
Mantelet of the same cloth,
Adorned with velvet,
Worn wrapped around;
They seem daughters of queens,
They seem Grecian statues,
As if in the rays of sunset
At peace they recline;
Rich Manila shawls,
White and cherry-coloured,
Crossed over their breasts
In chaste modesty;
Atop these they show off
Like glittering stars
Adornments and necklets
Of diamonds and pearls,
Pendants of filigree
And waxen broaches.

The girls from Camariñas dress
Like gleeful lasses,
Skirts of bright colours
To the calf of the leg,
Showing off black shoes
Over white stockings.
Blouses striped all over
In blues and reds,
With fringes that tumble
To the swing of their hips.
To play the tambourine
There's no better than these girls,
Who are from Camariñas,
Made of salt and cinnamon.

Those from Cee, Our Lady of Carmel!
What beautiful sweet faces!
When they go all flushed
In the merry bustle,
Each look from their eyes
Wounds like a hundred darts.
There are no hands better groomed,
No hands as pale and small
As those they show pretending
They don't want them to be seen.

Those from Laxe, they're the girls
And oh, such girls!
From the moment they appear,
Boys doff their alpine caps;
'Cos they're lively with mischief
And they're such hearty girls.
As dancers… no others
Can match their prowess,
For to dance they'd even high-step
On the screen of a sieve;

And yet, when called to prayer,
They're the first to pray…
They grant the world what's the world's
And to the church what is the church's.

Those girls from Noia are like
The gracious girls of Rianxo,
With their tiny dainty feet,
Their hair in curls,
Their dark beauty spots
And their prickly tongues,
That have such a bite, oh,
As if they were pepper!

They arrive discreetly,
With just a touch of snob,
For they know so much of
Lineage and noblesse
(Well, where're we're from that's
Just how God made us),
The beautiful daughters
Of a very fussy town,
Who wherever they show up
Seem to say, 'Holy moley!
Do we trump or don't we
All the girls around here?'
Whether they do or don't
It's not my place to tell you,
It wouldn't be wise,
It would be far too frank.
Enough to say that together
In the church portal
They look more beautiful
Than a bouquet of white lilies,
Fresher than lettuce,
Tastier than strawberries.

Whether they're from Rianxo,
From Redondela,
Camariñas or even Laxe,
From Laxe or Ponteareas,
They were all so pretty,
Pretty were these girls,
Even the hardest of beings
Would give his heart for them…
That's why they melted,
As if made of butter,
The guys that stood near them,
Young gallants of the party,
Fishers from the seas
Who'd come to our Lady
Because she'd saved them
From shipwreck in a storm.
But though saved at sea
They'll not be on earth;
Sailors, sailors,
Here too there are storms
That drown tender hearts
Before they're even offered
And though our Lady hears drownings
At sea amid the waves' roar,
She doesn't hear lovers,
Who drown with glee.

II

Like a bouquet of flowers,
Muxía of the steep crags
Is scattered with pink
Along its white shore,
With so many sails
That glitter in the sands,
With so many folks on the run
Who dash and whirl
To the sound of bagpipes reeling
And the pop of fireworks,
Some are selling lemonade,
Some refreshing water,
Some sweet anise liqueur
With almond cookies,
Over there there's watermelon
With mouth-watering plums,
While in the midst a blind man
To the happy sound of tambourine
Strums a tune on the guitar
To make the girls dance.
Blessed be Our Lady of the Barque,
May she be blessed forever!
My miraculous Lady,
In whose name so many have fun!
All come to visit her,
All go down to see her
In her gilded boat,
In her tiny boat,
That holds two angelic figures,
Two sweet angels that row.
There she arrived miraculously
On a ferry of stone.
There, for God willed it,
She'll always be adored.

The stone bobs and rocks,
Acts as her sentinel
And while men sleep,
She bestows her adoration
With her church-bell choir
That peels in the distance,
To which the sea answers
With humble roars.
When the bells ring out
And the music echoes,
As if in heaven, amid the naves
Of the jam-packed church,
When the fireworks explode
In the air and fresh voices
Rise in space, with sweet bagpipes
Mixed with drummed cadence,
Then the stone rocks,
So glad and so happy
That though a hundred people
Leap up and jump on it,
As if it were a young woman,
Light as a feather,
Happy as Easter,
It leaps up and jumps with them.
Gifts then shower down,
As well as offerings,
That the pilgrims bring her
In adorned little baskets,
Before the blessed Lady,
At the feet of Heaven's Queen,
And they sing out now
When they bid her farewell:
'Our Lady of the Barque
Has a canopy of stone:
You could have one of gold,
My Lady, just say the word.'

7

'Twas on a Sunday,
'Twas in late afternoon,
With the sun going down
Through the pine groves,
With white clouds
Shadow of the angels,
With little butterflies
That beat their wings,
With a rhythm
Meek and smooth,
Crossing
Celestial spaces,
Foreign worlds
Cleaved by rays of sun,
Rich treasures
Of gold and diamond.
I tramped mountains,
Crests and valleys,
I tramped plains
And emptiness:
I tramped across ditches,
I tramped over oceans,
Kept my feet dry
And never got tired.

Night overtook me,
Brilliant night,
With a frail moon
Made of jasper,
And I went with it
On the road ahead,
With twinkling stars

To guide me,
For the path
Was one they knew.

Later dawn
With its colours
Made of roses
Arrived to light me;
And I saw then,
Between the leaves
Of elms and pines,
Was nestled
A small white house
With dovecote,
Where sweet doves
Settled and flew.
From the cottage
Gentle songs came,
Inside it the ruckus
Of young men flirting
With sweet young ladies
From the villages nearby.
All is contentment,
All is enjoyment,
While the millstone
Thrums and thrums,
Grinds and grinds,
Spits out and spits out
Just as it pleases,
Keeping time.

There's no place
Cheers me more
Than that mill
In the chestnuts,
Where young girls are,

Where young men are,
Who so richly know
How to unwind.
Where they spin it out
Until they're tired,
Young and old,
Kids and adults,
And though no one asked
Me to go down there,
For in this house
I knew no one,
I was at the mill
Of my godfather,
I went on the wind,
I arrived on the air.

8

A portly bagpiper
Dressed up in fine silk,
Like a total prince,
Affectionate and witty,
First among young men,
Urbane without peer,
He had a way of singing
At the break of dawn:
'My little bagpipe
Can sweet-talk any girl.'

He always came to town
With the air of a young lord,
With imposing brio always
And accompanied by a drum,
And when he blew in the bagpipe,
He exhaled so softly,
Then he'd burst into song
There at the break of dawn:
'My little bagpipe
Can sweet-talk any girl.'

The girls were wild for him,
All were swooning at him,
If he was near, they smiled,
If he was far, they cried.
Oh no! They didn't notice
In all his flowery ways
That he had a way of singing
There at the break of dawn:
'My little bagpipe
Can sweet-talk any girl.'

As the procession moved past,
Underneath a fig tree,
How many single young girls
Murmured 'I love you!' to him…
And he let his bagpipe answer,
To enchant them completely,
Then he'd burst into his song
There at the break of dawn:
'My little bagpipe
Can sweet-talk any girl.'

The girls danced captivated
And ran right after him,
Blindly, blindly not noticing
The brambles circling them;
Poor butterflies, they were after
The light that would burn them,
For he had a way of singing
There at the break of dawn:
'The sound of my little bagpipe
Can sweet-talk any girl.'

At the fairs, such contentment!
Such laughs in the sewing bees!
All the girls were swooning,
They proved his thinking right;
And he who thirsted for lovers
Wanted to sweet-talk them all.
When he saw them weeping later,
He sang at the break of dawn:
'If they weren't already crazy,
They wouldn't answer my song.'

9

The priest once warned me
It's a mortal sin…
But it's deep in my spirit,
How can I shake it off?

The spindle can spin and spin,
Night and day,
And think and think it over,
Argue and argue with you…

You always reap what you sow,
Till the cup overflows,
For where the devil's at work
It's said his work's never done.

I yell even louder, 'Betrayer!
Get lost, you devil!'
But the fiendish demon
Awaits me then and now.

More I worry, the more I'm sorry,
All is lost!
For Jacinto doesn't want me,
Not single, nor married.

In one way or another,
If truth be told,
I wished to sorely tempt him,
As the enemy tempts me.

That it's a sin... my sweet soul!
Why is it that
You can't, if you're a girl,
Seek what you most desire?

I can't find a way out
Or make sense of it all,
It drives me to bitterness,
These ever wicked thoughts.

They say you're like a hawk
Without feathers;
If it's true, my hawk,
You've my heart in your claws!

You might call me
A crackpot;
But rather than lie tarnished
I crave the sear of the fire.

If others look at you as I do,
My love,
They'll not call me crazy,
Even you can't cause me pain.

I saw him on a misty morning,
At the wee spring,
Sleeping under an oak,
Atop the wet grass.

I slowly came closer,
Right to his side,
And sighed as meekly
As a welcome breeze.

And his mouth was half open,
Like that of a child,
Who wakes watching the sky,
Lying down in the rye.

And his curly locks
Tumbled over him,
As sheep in flocks
Fall on flowers as they open.

My God, what a flower he was,
Opening like that…
And the grasses right then
Held him so close!

What frost, what mist,
Refreshed him!
Even the oak tree
Put its branches around him!

While I gazed at him
He turned over
And I thought I'd be drowned
By the beat of my heart.

It beat and beat, beating,
Unable to stop,
But I said trembling:
'I must speak to him now.'

And again he turned over
So very slowly,
Oh and I dashed away,
Fleet-footed down the path!

Afterward I cried, how I cried,
In utter shame,
I said, 'If he doesn't fall for me
I'll never speak to him again.'

And he didn't fall for me, no,
Drat it all!
While my heart still
Loves him even if it's a sin.

And he frequents other girls
So happily
And I, with each pretty one,
Hold him in my heart.

Whether he likes it or not
He's with me
And in the end and finally
The enemy tempts me with him.

You always reap what you sow,
Till the cup overflows!
For where the devil's at work
It's said his work's never done.

As such, though the priest said
It's a sin,
Even though he does me no good,
I'll never let him go.

10

'I loved you so much, girl,
I had for you such great love,
That for me you were moon,
Pale dawn and bright sun;
Clear water in fresh springs,
Rose of God's garden,
The breath in my chest,
The life of my heart!'
So I did tell you one day,
On the way to San Lois,
Weighed down by anguish,
All ardent with passion,
While you listened to me
Pulling petals from a flower
So I wouldn't see your eyes
That reflected betrayal.
After you told me 'yes,'
As a token of your love,
You gave me a wee carnation,
That I held in my heart.
Dark damned carnation
That wounds me with pain!
But in crossing the river,
The carnation sank!…
I hope your path's as straight
As that of the carnation.

11

Bells of Bastabales,
When I hear you call,
I die of yearnings.

I

When I hear you call,
Dear bells, beloved bells,
I can't help but start to cry.

When I hear you in the distance,
I think it's for me you're calling
And I ache in my heart.

I ache wounded, pining,
For once my life was whole
And today my life's but half.

Only half they left me,
Those over there who brought me,
Those over there who robbed me.

You'll not rob me again, traitors,
Oh, what a senseless love!
Oh, a love completely senseless!

And now with love long gone,
The yearnings have come…
And consume me with grief.

II

There at the break of dawn,
I climbed to the hilltops,
Fleet-footed, fleet-footed.

Like a scrambling crab,
To hear my beloved bells
Sound their first peel.

The first sight of daybreak
Brought me by sweet breezes,
To see me more consoled.

To see less of my tears,
They bring me it on their wings,
Frolicking and rumbling.

Rumbling and shuddering
Through the thick foliage,
Through the green leaves of the trees.

And across the green meadow,
Over the flat plains,
Frolicking and frolicking.

III

Slowly, slowly,
As the afternoon wanes I walk,
On the path from Bastabales.

Path of my contentment;
And as long as the sun's out,
On a stone I sit down.

And from my seat I watch
How the moon is rising,
How the sun is setting.

How the sun sets, how it hides,
While the moon races
Not knowing where it's headed.

Where it's headed so alone,
Without us who sadly watch it,
It won't speak to us, nor hear us.

For if it could hear and speak to us,
So many things it would say,
So many things it would tell us.

IV

Each star, its diamond;
Each cloud, white plume,
The moon moves sadly past.

As it moves, it lights up
Plains, meadows, peaks, rivers,
Where day is waning.

The day wanes and dark night
Descends, descends slowly
From mountains of green.

Of green and foliage,
Dotted with small springs
Beneath the shade of branches.

Of branches where sing
The little songbirds,
Who wake up at dawn.

Who at night go to sleep
And let crickets sing
That appear with the shadows.

V

The wind races, the river flows,
Clouds race, clouds race
Along the path to my home.

My home, my abode:
They vanish and I'm bereft
Of company or friend.

I stay contemplating
Chimney smoke from the wee houses
Among which I live, sighing.

Come the night… day departs,
The bells chime out far away
The notes of the Angelus.

It is the call to prayer,
But I don't pray, for it seems
The sobs that drown me
Pray for me in my stead;
Bells of Bastabales,
When I hear you call,
I die of yearnings.

12

I

I saw you on a clear night,
The eve of Saint John,
Placing fresh grasses
To infuse in spring waters.
And so beautiful you were,
A rose in its bower,
That with fresh mist
Is gilded all over.
That's why, love-stricken,
With a gentle sigh
I threw my loving arms
Round your waist.
And you with sweet eyes
And even sweeter words,
Enchantress, you lured me
Into sweet solace.
All the wee stars
Way up there in space
Smilingly watched us
With delicate light.
They were, oh, witnesses
To that sigh of yours
Which was met by my own
With equal love!
But later with other men
More majestic and gallant
(But no, who cannot love you more
Than I did, no one can),
With them too, them too, dear lass,
You were one to converse

In the shade of the willows,
Where the procession path ends.
That's why I sang out to you
In sad solitude,
When, poor me, I saw you
Exchanging with them:
'Be careful, my sweet girl,
Of exactly what you exchange,
For where so many spit,
  Mud is formed.'

II

  How sad you look now!…
How sad, girl, you are!…
All your vivid colours,
Where, sweet girl, did they go?
Your gaze serene,
Your gentle song,
Where, sweet girl, where
Do you expect to find them?
I didn't see you, sweet girl,
On the Eve of Saint John,
Laying fresh grasses
To infuse in spring waters.
I didn't see you fresh
As the rose in its bower,
How wrinkled your face was
From all your sobbing.
Now in the pain you ache from,
Honour's what you seek,
Sweet honour that you lost,
But who will give it back?
I'd love, my dear girl,
To give it back to you,

For all the good I felt for you
It hurts now to see you sad.
As for saying, if I were to say
How pure you are, my child,
They'd answer me in smiles
Just to make fun of me:
'You know very well, Frankie,
Frank from Pombal,
That where so many spit,
Mud is formed.'

13

Blessed Saint Anthony,
Give me a man,
Even if he slays me,
Even if he scorns me.

Oh my holy Saint Anthony,
Give me a little man,
Even one small
As a grain of corn.

Give him to me, my saint,
Even if his feet limp
And his arms are mangled.

A woman with no man,
Blessed saint,
Is a body without soul,
Feast without grain!

Oar that rows crooked,
Where you want it to go
It stalls like a cabbage stalk.

But with a little man,
Our Lady of Carmel,
There's no crowd that shows up
Just to have fun!

Eagle-toed or knock-kneed,
It's always good to have a man
To solve the problem.

I know one that I covet
From when first I saw him,
Graceful in his body,
Flushed and ruddy.

Flesh sweet as butter
And words as soft
As they are lies.

I pine for him all day,
Pine all night,
Thinking of his eyes
Colour of sky.

But he, so adept,
Knows love very well,
But little of marrying.

Make him, my Saint Anthony,
Come to my side,
To get married to me,
An unmarried girl.

I have as dowry
A spoon of iron,
Four of boxwood.

A tiny little brother
Who already has teeth,
An ancient old cow
That doesn't give milk...

Oh my precious saint,
Make it come true,
Just as I ask you!

        Blessed Saint Anthony,
Give me a man,
Even if he slays me,
Even if he scorns me.

Eagle-toed or knock-kneed,
It's always good to have a man
To solve the problem.

14

Over there atop
Of the fresh mountain,
That is covered gaily
In green grasses,
Dark girl
Dressed in white
Seems a cloudlet
Lost on the mountain.
That spins, that races,
That turns, that passes,
That rolls and gently,
Serenely halts.

All wrapped up she is
In the mist that leaps
From the streams that bubble
In the raucous cascade.
Standing on the tip
Of the shadowy crag,
Immobile as a virgin
Of stone she is seen.
Her bonnet of linen
Has flown to the winds,
Her tresses all tangled
Are fanned by the air.
The flapping ends
Of the silk of her shawl
Look from afar
Like angel wings.
And the afternoon breezes
Playing with them
Move them with the grace

That an angel would have.
I think – crazy
Me! – they're calling to me,
When I see them waving
In the tangle of green,
But oh, if my eyes
Don't betray and trick me,
For I go and, fleeing,
She hides in the fog,
Hides once again,
In the shade of the pines,
And hidden she sings
Sweet little songs,
That enflame, that wound,
Wound with the love
That grows deep
In my heart.

How shapely, how pretty,
How fresh, how pale
God did make her, sweet girl
Of the green mountain!
How beautiful she looks,
What tears, what sighs!
Singing, smiling,
Awake, asleep!
Oh, if her father
Would bestow her to me!
Oh, I'd feel no more
Grief in the world!
Oh, if I had her
With me as my lady,
I would dress her in finery,
I would give her shoes.

15

Goodbye, rivers, goodbye, springs,
Goodbye, trickling streams;
Goodbye, all I see before me:
Who knows when we'll meet again?

Oh my home, my homeland,
Soil where I was raised,
Little garden that I cherish,
Fig trees I grew from seed.

Meadows, rivers, woodlands,
Pine groves bent by wind,
All the chirping little songbirds,
Home I cherish without end.

Mill nestled between the chestnuts,
Nights lit brightly by the moon,
Tremor of the little bells,
My parish chapel's tune.

Blackberries from the wild vines
I picked to give my love,
Narrow trails between the corn-rows,
Goodbye, forever goodbye!

Goodbye, glory! Goodbye, gladness!
I leave the house where I was born,
Leave my village so familiar
For a world I've never seen.

I'm leaving friends for strangers,
Leaving prairies for the sea,
Leaving all that I love dearly...
Oh, if I didn't have to leave!...

But I'm poor and I'm unlucky
And my land is not my own,
Even the path you walk
Is borrowed if
To privation you are born.

So it is I have to leave
The precious garden I've so loved,
Warm hearth of my dwelling,
The new trees I planted there,
Spring outside the cabin door.

Goodbye, goodbye, I'm going,
All you grasses over the graves,
Where my father lies deep buried,
Grass I've often leaned to kiss,
Sweet soil where we were raised.

Goodbye, Our Lady of Assumption,
As white as a seraphim,
I carry you in my heart:
Please pray to God for me,
Virgin Mary heaven-bound.

Far off I hear them, far away,
The bells over in Pomar,
That ring for me, oh, heartache,
They'll ring for me no more!

Far off I hear them, far away...
Each peel pierces with its ache:
I go alone, without companion...
Oh my home, goodbye! Goodbye!

Goodbye too, my beloved...
Goodbye forever it may be!...
I cry as I bid you farewell
From the shoreline of the sea.
Don't forget me, home beloved,
Though I die of loneliness...
So many leagues across the sea...
My sweet abode! My hearth!

16

I clearly saw the owl there
On top of that great crag:
I'm not afraid of you, owl,
Owl, I'm not afraid of you!

I

One night, night dark as
All the sadness that I bear,
Night daughter of the shadowy
Wings that fears extend;
Hour when the roosters crow,
Hour when the winds sigh,
When witches dance, dance,
Alongside the fiercest devil,
Uprooting green oaks,
Doors and shingles shattered,
All of them dressed in white,
Their white hair clasped,
Against them the dogs howl
Prophesying a sad burial;
In the scant light there peer
Between thick gorse tangles,
Like lit candles,
Eyes of famished wolves
And the mountain brush
Murmurs quietly to itself
And the dry leaves strewn
By restless night breezes
Gather in whirlwinds
With extended shivering;

While heading to the church,
Alone with my thoughts,
At the fountain of Our Lady
Nestled by the cemetery,
After feeling a sigh
That left me breathless,
I clearly saw the owl there
On top of that great crag!

II

In goose-bumps
All my skin rose
And my hair on top
Stood up on end:
Drops of sweat ran
Streaming down my chest
And I trembled as does
Water, when the wind rises,
In the basin of the new fountain,
That always overflows.
That owl sat there unmoving,
As if it were the devil itself,
Looked me up and down
With its rapacious eyes,
That I feared were robbing me
When I first saw their glint.
They seemed to be of fire
And scorched me, so I felt;
I think they were red embers
From the fires stoked in hell,
That pierced me in the pupils
And went right to my heart.
There where I was remorseful
For my sins of love...

Oh, whoever's felt such love
Can never feel at peace!

It rained as if God had water
And all the winds, they blew
And everything so soaking wet
I didn't dare to walk the road,
For the owl, who stares and stares,
Awaits me on that crag.
But I recalled the Virgin Mary
That I always bear with me,
I prayed her a Hail Mary
And regaining my breath anew,
Like birds far out at sea,
I cross the stream by swimming
And I race over the wall,
Leap beneath the doorway
And from there I yell
With all the strength I have:
*'I'm not afraid of you, owl,
Owl, I'm not afraid of you!'*

17

Little breezes, breezy breezes,
Little breezes of my land;
Little breezes, breezy breezes,
Little breezes, lift me home.

Without my home I cannot live,
Cannot live in happiness,
For wherever I want to go,
In thick shadow I am dressed.
A thick cloud cloaks me,
Pregnant with its storms,
Pregnant with loneliness,
It poisons my life.
Lift me, lift me, little breezes,
Like a tiny brittle leaf,
For I too am left dry
By the burning heat.
Oh, if you don't soon lift me upward,
Little breezes of my land,
If you don't lift me, little breezes,
No one will recognize me soon.
For the fever that eats me
Will slowly consume me
And will even break out
In betrayal in my own heart.

I once glowed as crimson
As the colour of a plum,
Today I've lost all colour
Like wax figures in the church,
As if a vampire sucking
Had drunk up all my blood.

I'll end up just as withered
As the rose in winter is,
Listless I'll become then
And go darker even still
Than the darkest Moorish baby,
Whose mother is dark too.

Lift me, lift me, little breezes,
Lift me to where they wait:
A mother who sheds tears for me,
A father who without me cannot breathe,
A brother for whom I'd give
The blood inside my veins
And a lover to whom my soul
And life I've promised.
If you don't soon lift me upward,
Oh, I'll die of unhappiness,
Alone in a strange country
Where they light on me as strange,
Where no matter where I look
Everything says I don't belong.

Oh my poor house I call home!
Oh my ruddy Galician cow!
Rams, that bleat up in the mountains,
Coo of doves in threshing yards,
Whoops of young gallants dancing,
Clack of the castanets,
Ca-ca-ca-ra-ca of the spoons,
Swoosh of the tambourines,
Drumbeat of all the drums,
Little bagpipe, Galician bagpipe,
You're not here to gladden me
As you call out *muiñeira* dances!
Oh, if only I were a wee bird
With light and speedy wings!

Oh, I'd fly so quickly,
Crazed with happiness,
To sing at daybreak
In the fields of my land and home!
I'd leave this very minute,
Like an arrow I'd be gone,
Unafraid of night's shadows,
Unafraid of blackest night.
And rain or wind wouldn't stop me,
I wouldn't stop for wind or rain,
I'd fly and fly above
Until my native land I saw.
But alas, I am no songbird
And I'll go on dying of my pain,
Racked with tears already
And broken in my sighs.

 Sweet lovely Galician breezes,
You banish every ache,
You enchant all the waters,
Lovers of the woods,
Music of the green stalks
Of corn on our own plains,
Cheerful little companions,
Gusts that gather at every feast,
Carry me on your wings
Like a dry little leaf.
Don't let me die here,
Little breezes of my land,
Though I think that even dead
I'll still sigh to go there.
I still think, breezy breezes,
That when I'm dead and gone
And off there in the graveyard,
With earth heaped over me,
You'll pass by in the depths of night

Rustling the dry leaves
Or whistling frightfully
Between the bleached white skulls,
Even after sweet death greets me,
Little breezes of my land,
I'll cry out to you: 'Little breezes,
Little breezes, lift me home!'

18

To Camilo Álvarez de Castro,
preceptor at Salamanca Cathedral

I

Ruddy as the golden sun,
Gorgeous as the fresh rose,
She walked on the lovely mountain
With her white foot unshod…
A snowflake fallen,
Sparkling in the light of day,
That's what her white foot seemed.

Her long tresses tumbled
And when winds played in them
Wavelets of gold formed
All down her white back;
As full and ripe
As stalks of grain they were, thought
He who watched them far away.

The colours of the sea
Glinted in her sleepy eyes
And eyes more gentle, clearer,
No one could ever find;
No one sees them without loving
The steadfast heart
Visible through them.

She carried her soul on her face
And laughter on her gentle lips,
Small waters that the wind ripples
Pushed to the bottom when calm.

Just as a gallant hand
Slowly takes hold of her
Around her tiny waist.

Just as the warm breeze
Races between the willows,
She follows, racing too,
Along an enchanting riverbank.
Gently and peacefully there
A spring freshet poured out
On the skirt of the mountain.

II

Frank, pure, without guile,
She sings, sings aloud,
At the foot of the green brambles
Washing her white sheets.
To the sound of the vain murmurs
Risen in the little spring,
She washes, washes, in the fountain.

Near her the songbirds
Chunter in happiness,
The wind revels for her
With its brothers, the breezes.
The shepherds, poor souls,
Sing her the sweet *a... la... lala...*,
That the language of love speaks.

She listens honestly.
But she replies with sighs,
For she harbours in unknown places
Longings from who knows when?
The sheets she keeps washing

And after hanging them she lies
In a little field of green.

Then in the passing stream
She lets fall a serene tear,
Child of the hidden longing
That pierces her breast.
For she's ablaze with love,
This one who is fresh as a rose,
As loving as she is pretty.

Her friends are arriving,
One girl after another comes laden,
Jars of glazed pottery
They set amid the pebbles.
The sweet waters fall in murmurs,
White bubbles rise up,
The girls sing… sing.

The stars continue fleeing,
The thick fog dissipates,
The small flowering bushes
Come back into view.
The clear sun goes on rising
Across the firmament,
Clean, brash and glad.

All and everything exudes
The scent of spring
And up there in the blue sphere
A blaze of glory lights up.
Yet the girl awaits nothing
But the heartache, alas,
That wells in her breast.

The songs make her feel lonely,
Her desires make her cry
And with eyes full of tears
She thinks of her native land.
There could be no grief sadder,
No melancholy darker
Than that which grows amid strangers.

Songbirds, green meadow,
White moon and burning sun,
Every consolation is impotent
In such disconsolate despair.
All contentment is clouded
By the bottomless ache
That in her heart abounds.

So the beautiful young girl
Left the gay beloved fountain,
Just like a sad lamb
That trembles from whining pain.
She goes sadly, goes crying,
While they yell at her with gusto:
'Hillbilly! Hayseed girl!'

And she, who felt so strange,
Hurt in what she most loved,
Could not accept being insulted
And thus she shyly answered:
'I am from the mountains,
I'm a mountain girl,
Oh yes, I am and I don't care who says so.'

19

Roll on, river, roll on, river,
As you gently burble past,
Roll on, roll on between flowers
Colour of marble and gold,
To which your sweet lips in passing
Tell such sweet things.
Roll on, roll on, they don't know
That you're going to endless sea,
For if they did, then, poor flowers,
How they'd weep for you!
If you only knew what strangeness,
If you just knew what suffering
Since I've lived far from him
My heart has felt!
Longings grip me strongly
And they rise to torment me,
Even more demons choke me
If I try to shake them off.
Oh, who besides the flowers,
Seeing you so far away,
Goes down to the green shore
On the banks of the Carril!

Roll on, roll on, so peaceful,
As you gently burble past,
Out to the salty waters,
Out to ocean without end;
And carry these tear droplets
If you happen to pass by there,
Very close to my beloved,
Very close to my lifeblood.
Oh, if I were but a teardrop,

I could go, dear love, to you!…
It would make me a trail
On which to travel, oh, woe is me!
If the sea only had verandas
From which to see you in Brazil;
But the sea has no verandas,
Oh my love, where then can I go?

20

'Hey, sweet baby boy, hey,
Who's there to give you milk
If your mama's off to the mill
And your dad to cut firewood?
I'd give it to you, my jewel,
With unending love I'd do,
Until it overflowed, my saint,
Until you wished no more,
Until I saw you sleeping
With that perfect little mouth
Smiling so repletely
At such an udderful.
But oh, may night look after you!
But oh, may night attend!
Even if I have two well-springs,
These well-springs cannot feed you.
Now, sweet baby boy, now
How you'll cry for milk!
With nothing here to warm you,
With nothing to help you sleep,
So alone, alone you're left
Like a sickly lamb awake,
Quivering, oh unlucky one,
As only lambs can shake.
Without coverlet to cover you,
In straw they lay you down
And snow and rain fall over you
From cracks in the broken roof.
And the passing wind whistles
Through the badly pointed stones
And like a sharpened knife
Pierces freely your small bones.

Oh, when will your mother come!
Oh, when will she come to you!
To find you, wee baby boy,
Cold even as the snow,
To cry until breath is gone,
Little wind-shattered rose...
Oh, it would be better, baby,
If to your mother you'd not been born!
Woe to the children of the poor
Who are born for such grief.'

    That's what Rosa uttered
In the midst of darkest night,
At the foot of a dark doorway,
All chapped with cold.
Accompanied by the murmuring
Through the thicket of oaks
Of the river's roiling waters
And the shriek of the storm.
The sky was all in shadow,
The earth in mourning too,
And it seemed as if the ghouls
Were dancing in the trees
With bloodsucking enemies
And the brazen witches.

    Just then a wail so soft
Made itself felt in space,
Like a bagpipe reel
In the serenity of dawn;
Like a distant flute
When sun falls into the sea,
Its sound brought us on the wind
With the breezes of the shore.

In the midst of the dark hovel
That sad Rosa watched,
A pale light was seen
Like at the glint of dawn.
Scent of fresh roses
That the night air diffused,
As if every flower of spring
Had been gathered together.
Strange songs rang out,
Music rang out so gay;
Music, sounds and songs
Never heard before on earth.
At once, stunned, Rosa
Bit by bit drew close
And through a crack
Down on the floor she peeked.

Never before had human eyes
Seen what she saw just then
And if she didn't die afterward
It was not what God had willed.
In resplendent glory
Rays of love reflected
From the abandoned boy child,
All round his golden head;
And to make him happier
And to care more for him
Near his little feet were growing
Fresh branches of lilies.
He no longer slept poorly cradled,
Another bed they'd made for him,
The little angels with their wings
And the stars with their fire.
Clouds a rosy colour
Softly pillowed him,
He had for a blanket

A ray of full moon
And the Blessed Virgin, draped
In robes of innocence,
So that he'd not die from hunger
And full would fall to sleep,
She gives him manna from her breast,
Refreshment for his lips.

As long as the world continued,
Rosa would have watched,
To see so much enchanting glory
And so much true suspense;
But a distant voice is heard
Through the elms along the plain
That singing lovingly
Expresses itself like this:
'Now, baby, sweet babe, now
Soon I will give you milk,
Now, baby, sweet babe,
You'll soon not cry for it.'

This they sang. While
With the Virgin vanished
The wee angels, leaving
Thick night in their wake.
Already their steps were felt
Along the footpath;
They've leapt the gate already,
Already closed the latch…
The poor mother runs, runs,
For her babe is awaiting her;
But when she arrives, asleep
Is how she finds her baby son.
She says to him, meanwhile,
These words in kissing him:

'My jewel, my jewel,
My darling, my darling,
Whatever would become of you
If you'd not had a mama;
Who, my child, would wash you,
Who would give you food?'

'The ants would feed him
And the songbirds sustain him.'

So Rosa said and hid herself
In the thick swirl of mist.

21

I'm not saying a thing...
  But really!

I

  In this life there come to pass
Things that are so strange,
Such weird things come to happen
In this deceptive world;
Many old miracles,
New things to learn
And a lot of wild garlic
Pretending to be salad...
I'm not saying a thing...
  But really!

  A girl all dressed up,
Girl in fine shoes,
Who has working clothes
And party clothes;
Girl who has fun,
Girl so elegant
And he's poor, unlucky,
Like a sad spider.
I'm not saying a thing...
  But really!

  I see you, girl, in the corn,
I see you in the fenland,
Now in the thick pinewoods,
Now at the gentle bank

Of the river that racing
Moves between green stalks,
And I swear that you're alone,
That no one goes with you…
I'm not saying a thing…
But really!

Married, yes, you're married,
Yet you like to be seen
Dancing with unwedded girls
At festivals and jamborees,
On your lips there's laughter
And your eyes speak volumes
And in talking with them
They seem to leap out of you,
I'm not saying a thing…
But really!

When watching I watch you
So bright with your perfect hair,
Fooling with the young men
Until they're full of you,
And you later swearing
You're a woman unsullied,
You say that the others just
Can't hold a candle to you.
I'm not saying a thing…
But really!

And you, red-headed girl,
Modest and demure,
You speak so softly,
So gently you saunter,
You who look downward
So as not to see men's faces,
Pretend you don't understand

When they say words of love.
I'm not saying a thing...
But really!

You go in early morning
To Mass with the devout girls,
Then (you know the reason)
You slip away from them;
And if on the footpath
Alongside the vineyard,
Who knows what sort of people
You tarry with or don't?
I'm not saying a thing...
But really!

And you, striking gallant,
Full of sweet babble,
Rakish in your alpine cap,
Attired in rich leggings,
In boots so fine
And with patrician fingers,
When you go into the green hay
Saying you like to work there,
I'm not saying a thing...
But really!

You'll speak of love
And highfalutin things,
You'll fool around with the girls
As no one else has fooled;
You'll drink the barrel dregs
Till you're left speechless
And till with your sweat
You soak ungrateful earth...
I'm not saying a thing...
But really!

Even more things I see
That seem to me deceitful;
So much sun amid clouds
And stormy waters
That just pretend to be
A placid fountain,
It's a waste of time trying
To get water from a stone,
So I'm not saying a thing...
   But really!

II

In this life there come to pass
Things that are so strange,
Such weird things come to happen
In this deceptive world;
Many old miracles,
New things to learn
And a lot of wild garlic
Pretending to be salad...
I'm not saying a thing...
   But really!

As for drawing conclusions,
It sadly falls on me,
For that I've got experience
No one would dispute,
With my brow all wrinkled
And my hair gone white,
While some young guys today
Who are barely weaned...
I'm not saying a thing...
   But really!

It's no good for you, Frankie,
To live in the company
Of thoughtful years
Or blunt experience,
Nor to keep your eyes open
And use common sense,
For where you least suspect
It leaps out huge as a hare.
I'm not saying a thing...
    But really!

In the midst of darkest night,
They tell you night's bright;
And when the sea's serene
They say it's storm-tossed
And they confuse you so much
And make you so cowardly
That even if you wanted to speak
In keeping with God's will...
I'm not saying a thing...
    But really!

If you were French, old man,
If you were from far Australia,
If you dropped from the sun
Or from the pale stars,
With serious gravity
Maybe they'd ask you.
And you, all spooked,
Would quietly murmur:
I'm not saying a thing...
    But really!

And so, old pal,
If you don't study
Contemporary science,

That is clear as water,
Although with soot
It could also be compared,
Science works like that,
There's two sides to a coin.
I'm not saying a thing...
But really!

Without knowing why,
You'll see how well they mix,
Honourable and disreputable,
Harlots and the pious;
You'll see how they gather,
You'll see how they act;
While you mutter softly
As if you had an alibi.
I'm not saying a thing...
But really!

You'll see cherry colour
In what is emerald green
And those who all in blue
Claimed veins that course blue blood,
Their blood is red
As we moderns know;
What a joke that is
And vain as well...
So I'm not saying a thing...
But really!

You'll see such ruckus,
Such wild square dances,
Bagpipes with flutes,
Fifes with harps,
Scarlet woven capes
With white mantelets,

It's all a wild whirl
In a frenzied state,
I'm not saying a thing...
But really!

You'll think that this
Is all carnivalesque,
That there's one preacher too many
Here and a jacket missing,
That there they eat rabbit
Instead of zucchini
And they pipe on flutes when
They should ring bells...
I'm not saying a thing...
But really!

Take up, my old buddy,
Well-cherished science,
That wisely teaches
Such a rich mixing,
If you want to be wise
In things so strange,
Well, in such new things
Rank habits still fester...
I'm not saying a thing...
But really!

22

But however much he wished,
If wishing had its way,
He still carried sorrow
Deep in his heart.

I

Out there in serene evenings,
Out there in quiet afternoons,
Grief seems so much harder
Than it feels at soft dawn.

Out there in shady evenings,
Out there in dark afternoons,
Laughter is cut shorter
And misfortune's darker grey.

There is no peaceful evening
For those filled with remorse
And they're crushed more quickly
When night draws close.

II

I well know these secrets
That hide in the entrails,
That churn ever restless
In a thousand strange forms.

I well know these torments
That consume and devour,
Those that make the winds howl,
Those that gnaw as they cry.

And though now I sing smiling,
Though with gusto I now sing,
I've wept and wept as much
As the waters of a river.

I have had in days past
Deep grief and regrets
And I've wept tears as frigid
As the waters of the sea.

I've felt such deep loves
And such deep bitterness
That it was a fount of pain
Arisen amidst hard grief.

III

Now I laugh, now happy
I sing in the threshing yard,
Travelling where the wind blows
When I'm off to herd the cows.

Oh, now so serenely
I sleep alongside the springs,
I sleep by the creek banks,
I sleep on mountain peaks.

But however much he wished,
If wishing had its way,
He still carried sorrow
Deep in his heart.

23

Castilian lady of Castile,
So pretty and so patrician,
But you can be bestial
To those who serve you.
Do tell me, your ladyship,
Since you seem ungrateful,
If my humble actions
Give you indigestion,
For when I come near you
You spit ardent gall.
And that sharp pigeon glare
You get in your face,
Turning to shadowy night
A day that basks in sun.
In vain I attempt, lady,
To know why you mistreat me,
With your soul so patrician,
Though famously haughty,
But there's no reason to despise
Feeling so well loved
That even the stones, lady,
Will lie around to please you.
They say that in noble Castile
That's how Galicians are treated,
But Castile must realize,
Though it considers itself highly,
That torpid haughtiness is always
The child of bastard souls;
And in being so wise
You might not have realized
That when you fall off your pedestal
You sully yourselves in the mud.

And in calling yourselves noble
You'll defile yourselves in nobility,
Imitating those who in vanity
Bully everyone who is weak.
It would be better that you shut up,
For you are ungracious;
And preaching in the desert
Is not done where I'm from.
My guilt was in loving you
As no one had loved you,
For I'm from Galicia
And you are Castilian.
In peace, my lady, I'll leave you
With your haughty grace
And go to beautiful Galicia
Where you can't fathom, lady,
What awaits me,
For in Castile there is none:
Little fields of pretty roses,
Springs of fresh waters,
Shade on the banks of rivers,
Sun in glad mountains,
Faces born smiling
And that, smiling, love you
And that even in dying
Beatifically smile.
There, my lady, I'll be happy
Singing sweet *ala lalas*,
Under fronds of the fig tree,
Below green grapevines,
With those fresh young women
Whose lips are like honey
When they speak lovingly,
'You charmer,' they softly say.
As for all those ladies of Castile,
Most noble Castilian ladies,

I'd forget you in a minute,
Though you're so patrician.
In Galicia women feel pride,
But without being vain,
And it's easy with sweet soil
To forget bitter grounds.
I've left you, Castilian ladies,
In your own contempt poisoned,
In bitterness more bitter
Than an orange peel:
But I've got what can banish
That sour taste that burns,
I have a lady in Os Portos,
Another in Ribeiro de Avia,
And if the Os Portos girl is pretty,
Well, the Ribeiro girl is even better.

24

Sweet light of my eyes,
You'll know I'm alive
In this town where I've been
Since I arrived from Xinzo.
You'll know that, thanks to God
And the blessed scapular,
We didn't drown at sea
As Jason had worried,
Who is as brave, I admit,
As the huffing of a rooster.
You'll know that on arrival
They dressed me right up
In blue and yellow,
Like the other conscripts,
And then all together,
More than twenty-five of us,
We marched through the streets,
It was something to admire,
So majestic we were,
So white and clean.
If you'd only seen me, sweet light,
As I know other women saw me!
How they all stared at me,
Sidelong, on the sly…
And they were graceful young 'uns,
Saucy as all get-out,
But not one from this heart
Could draw even a sigh,
For your portrait was there,
Rubbing under my shirt.
For even if I'm not at your side,
Sweetheart whom I so esteem,

I didn't come alone, my precious,
For you came with me.

If you only knew how I ache,
If you knew how tormented I am
When I remember in the night
The way you sang to me!…
For I think of you when I'm awake,
I think of you when I'm sleeping,
I'm always thinking of you
As if you hold me spellbound.
It's as if you'd cast a spell on me
On Saint Martin's feast day,
Sticking your fingers
In the ball of bread dough.
But that's not why I feel it,
For even if you made me suffer
For leaving you, sweet light,
I would accept it like a lamb.

Nothing distracts me, sweet Rose,
From the ache I feel for you.
Day and night
This dear heart of mine
Talks constantly to you
Because I feel like speaking with you;
Our talk so loving
That I shiver to hear it.
Oh, what loneliness it brings me
And desolation and torment!
For when my heart talks to you
I too want to talk to you
As we did in happier days
Of our fine love.

How many times we swore
As you washed in the river
Beneath a towering willow,
Between laughter and sighs,
That never would we separate,
Never more would we be parted!
But such pledges
Like prickly roses
Lift lightly and scatter petals
When the cold winds blow.
Now, with the sea between us,
Goodbye, tender love!
You can't see me, nor I you
There at the riverside,
On those clear nights
At rest every Sunday.
The blackberries ripen
In brambles at the wayside,
The white flowers are born
Among stalks of corn.
The river passes no matter what,
Goldfinches sing in the branches,
All is green and leafy,
All is fresh and flowery,
Only we, Rose, are missing
From those green sweet fields.

My sweet Rose, console me
In this longing I feel.
Oh, how my memories kill me!
Oh, they'll be the end of me!
Say if your love for me is still strong,
Send me your news soon;
Tell me if you've kept the shawl
I gave you on Saint Benedict's Day,
That I bought one Thursday

For twelve bills and a bit.
Tell me too if you're using
The catechism of Christ to learn
To read, since you offered
To read my writings,
As in knowing a bit of the alphabet
You'd be able to figure them out.
I've already lost my fear
Of writing and of books,
Now I can jot letters clearly
That I myself admire,
As tall as stakes
And thicker or I'd be lying.

Goodbye, I send you my wishes
By means of Camilo;
Who knows what you'll think
Of these things I tell you?
But know, my sweet Rose,
Rose so sweetly scented,
That if you can read now, you'll
Understand the strokes I write,
I'll write you a letter
On the wings of a bird.

25

To Roberto Robert,
editor of La Discusión, who loves stories and Galician

I

Out in the most lovely spot
Of earth ever lit by sunlight,
Florid plain and delightful meadow
That to the fields of Eden compare;
There where the Sar rolls deep and solemn,
Its waters seem to sleep suspended
(So gentle its current in the oaky shadow),
There Hard-Luck Vidal was born.[1]

II

What calm! What light! What chatter!
Serene the lilt of songbirds rising
When sunrise peeks across the corral
Gilding fountains, lakes and fields!
What fresh breath! How sweet it is
To see the goats all flock together!
How fresh, how well dressed, are the women
Herding them to the village on market day!

---

[1] I realize that, strictly speaking, these octets aren't properly a poem, and could more appropriately be called a tale; but since I'm not planning at this point to write a book of stories in Galician, and because I've tried to depict village traditions in these poems, the use of octets is fitting, as they do shed light on one of our oldest, most familiar traditions. This patriarchal tale has always moved me, so I decided to make it into a poem, relying on the generosity of readers. So many of our village poor are never granted a taste of pork when an animal is butchered, and dream of the day when, like Vidal, they can tell their selfish neighbours, *'Too bad, I'll go share with someone else!'*

III

Never the murmur of the corrupt world,
Never the vanity of society's crazes,
None of the glow of empty honours
Have come to taint these idyllic places.
Blue sky, loving sun, fields in flower,
Blessed peace, no remorse or longing,
Hours that slow and gently wander,
That's how life and time pass by.

IV

Just as the first breeze of the morning
In the bosom of roses sleepily dozes
And just as it later wild and playful
Lifts into the most immense spaces
And drops again all in a murmur,
Over the roofs of the hovels it swirls,
On its wings it lifts the smoke of hearths
That in smudged waves attempts to rise!

V

And how at noon, far from the river,
Breezes, gusts, green meadows and copses
Repose all warm and listless
Like thirsty and weary travellers.
And how at evening a chilly breath
Suffused with mysterious trills of birds
Lightly passed and ventured near
And stirred air, river, tiny blossoms.

VI

Slowly but surely the hard-working folk
Return from their fields to tiny hovels,
While on the hearth the iron cauldron
Is full of rich greens on the simmer.
The beans and taters all together
With flecks of savoury salt pork steaming
Go well with friendly company and fullness
That heartens, welcomes and sustains.

VII

After the frugal dinner, in the loving
Glow of moonlight clear and gentle,
They rested in the yard together
With their grandad, famed for telling tales.
The rosary of the generous Virgin
They later prayed with solemn accents
And soul and body peacefully slept
Awaiting the glint of the new day.

VIII

'Twas peace and love and serene waters,
'Twas clear blue in the skies above,
There was no vanity that empoisons,
Nor vain craving, nor deadly torment,
Nor wild agitation, nor deep ache,
Nor lowly idle thoughts,
To smirch the sweet life full of laughter
That gently and meekly was so enjoyed.

IX

In that poor place, it could be seen
That some lived well and others not badly
And whoever was frail or overextended
Was helped and given a share.
No one felt dark hunger's hand
Oppress his heart too strongly,
Unless it was the unlucky creature
Whom they called Hard-Luck Vidal.

X

Orphan from birth, unhappy fate
Had handed him a legacy of misery,
With the dark desolation that haunts the poor,
No one on earth was so alone.
As when in the earthly dust can be seen
One chicken running after another,
He was poor and pained amidst the pained
And tormented among the sadly tormented.

XI

His house was a rickety stable, dark,
He had for a bed the humid earth,
As blanket, snow and blaring wind
That entered shivering through the cracks.
His was the living precarious and scant
Begged door to door by those past salvation,
That's what they told him, with the many taunts
That the poor in this world must endure.

XII

Never can the unhappy one say:
'This is mine!' for hard luck
Wouldn't even concede to grant him
A bit of warmth or tender feeling,
Nor a bit of love, for where there is
Poverty and desolation and misfortune,
Glory, luck and affection quickly pass
And at the threshold will not enter.

XIII

Always by luck Vidal had found
Broth and bread at someone's poor hearth,
Though no other charity to him was extended,
He had no right to expect any more.
Even if he'd been born for better things
And other ways to eat and enjoy,
He had to scrabble just to secure
A bit of boiled cabbage and a crust of bread.

XIV

Such was the story told by the prudent
With parsimony conscientious and grave
And they eagerly quoted wise proverbs
That all sound like 'Never sow on hard ground.'
So of the main dish Vidal never tasted,
For healthy moderation is never wasted
Or so the folks in power said
As they sat back and munched their fill.

XV

When the time came to slaughter the hog,
How congenial was the waft of charcoal
From swept threshing yards at morning's glow!…
What happy smoke between elm and fig trees
Carried the scent of pork through the air!
What chattering girls with their sleeves rolled!
What traffic between trough and kitchen!
And on the hearth what flames! What roaring fire!
What a rich and bountiful fry-up sizzles!

XVI

Liver with onions fried till golden,
With a small leaf of scented bay,
Even the dead would be restored to life
Eating morsels so rich, tender and tasty.
Pork loin in gravy with a tempting aroma
And the blood for blood sausages so juicy
Brimming in the shining cauldron,
Enticing them to stuff the savoury links.

XVII

The scene so pleasant and gratifying
Was repeated all around the village
With din and laughter and sheer contentment,
That such an event deserves.
But to torment him even more,
In the hovel of Vidal alone there was
Neither pig, nor sausages, nor abundance,
For all was cloudy and misfortune.

XVIII

On the cold stones of his hearth he sat
And watched all the bustle around him,
Accompanied by darkest solitude:
No one invited him to feast on pork,
For he was poor Vidal and was forgotten
And the sight of a poor man would be disturbing,
So between sighs, he repeated:
'If only I were rich for just one day!'

XIX

He had these desires almost daily,
But – sad fate! – they were never fulfilled
And all of them, all were full of misery
As year after year incessantly passed.
Old Vidal he was already and the hard skies
Of dark suffering could hurt him no more,
Still Vidal had never tasted pork
And no one invited him to partake.

XX

The tradition when it came time to taste
Was for neighbours to trade with neighbours
(Even today this custom resurges),
But no one called Vidal their neighbour,
For it would be an undignified and silly reversal
To give where nothing could be returned
And because of it, Vidal, poor sucker,
Never touched blood sausage, unlucky guy.

XXI

But oh cunning world! Perfidious world!
Who can trust in your steps and turns?
Who could prove themselves so stupid
To claim that night cannot turn to day?
Who in time so short and fleeting
Could say to those who knew Vidal
That such a sad and humble creature
Could bask in waves of fortune's thrall?

XXII

And so it was!... The all-seeing one
Above our huge transparent sphere
Amidst the scintillating stars in orbit
Had compassion on Vidal.
The slow forgetting of the powers had veered
And realized the agony of Vidal
And with an arm mysterious and powerful
Changed reckless fate in one fell swoop.

XXIII

And so there entered Vidal's door,
As a fat creek bursts into parched fields,
An inheritance from beyond Cadiz
That the poshest gentleman would envy.
The gold in the strongbox shone in his eyes,
Made him delirious and laugh and run cold,
His luck was of such great dimensions
His heart, in seeing, could hardly hold.

XXIV

He wept, smiled, kissed the earth
That was still damp from all his plaints,
And all the luck that humanity holds
Brimmed ardently from his heart.
Steadying himself, to his knees he sways
Seeing fortune so unmatched appear
And to God he bows and fervently prays
And adores his portentous mystery.

XXV

His duty over, Vidal recovered
From such a deep and pleasant surprise,
He washed, spruced up and composed himself,
With the grace of God now at his side.
He much admired himself so well dressed,
He felt at last like a gallant young rake
And though he was bald as an eagle,
It was as if his hair were dark and curly.

XXVI

'Hey, friend,' they call him, what a change!
When before they'd say 'Vidal!' with scorn;
And they look at him with pleasant faces
Where once they'd turned their face away.
So happy now they were to see him,
So many people crowded around him
And some would even dare to say
'Twas as a saint that he'd returned.

XXVII

How sad the face of human poverty
That is born amid sighs and pain
And how it can arrive at beauty when wealth
Appears to us with its laughing gaze,
Money brings its charm and kindness,
Even a God would become the devil
If assuming the figure of a banker
He raked in money and more money.

XXVIII

These are mysteries… they confound me
And in vain I propose to explain them;
But Vidal, philosopher to the bone,
Although he'd never learned in books,
Learned on his own from the world around him
And such changes in people were no surprise!
In his thick head he'd already guessed it
When he'd eagerly dreamed of being rich.

XXIX

So he received with courtesy
Acclaim, gift and compliment,
That one after another humbly paid him,
Vile scum of human sentiment.
He understood their petty grovelling
And no vain or torpid thought
Did he hold against such folk, oh no!
He thought long and hard on his revenge.

XXX

One morn from a blessed and loyal subject
A hog he purchased, magnificent hog!
So snow-white, so groomed and rotund
No neighbour had ever seen its like.
It was short of leg, its back so straight,
And round it was from head to tail,
Its hide so shimmered with its fat
It looked to be made of butter.

XXXI

'Praise the Lord!' 'May God bless you!'
'May Saint Anthony keep you!' they exclaimed
As, at a snail's pace, the huge hog
And its owner Vidal solemnly passed.
All made an effort to speak to Vidal,
Already envisioning the pig at slaughter,
For they weren't folk to lose out on a mouthful
Dead and salted at the hands of Vidal.

XXXII

Later the bellow of the unhappy beast
That suffered the deathblow from the knife
Was heard to split the air of the village,
Bit by bit the throat went mute.
Its final sigh sounded in a strident noise,
The blood ran, the butcher poured sweat
And in that solemn and critical moment
The pig was life and world and thought.

XXXIII

The dead body lies sprawled over there,
With an onion in its gaping mouth
(As if the unlucky pig is still eating),
But don't feel badly, it's only sleeping
The sad sleep of the unsuspecting,
For the fires of hell it will never feel,
Nor glory either, nor burning purgatory,
It'll sleep unfeeling in eternal rest.

XXXIV

It isn't just that Vidal is happy,
The sweet smell of pork drives him nuts,
For of all pigs ever born it was a marvel,
The one laid out before his eyes.
True satisfaction, true contentment,
In all who watched, glowed in their faces,
Which spoke loud in silent language:
'Yes, that is one hefty pig!'

XXXV

But Vidal shut himself up with the hog
While chattering folk just stared...
They were knocked for a loop, stunned, trumped,
For never before in that place had it happened
And some were swearing eternal war
At how the world was turned upside down,
For never ever had any neighbour
Had a door slammed so hard in their face.

XXXVI

There arose a disgruntled rumble,
But Vidal was deaf to all their noise;
He spent the whole night shut away
And early at dawn on the following day,
Loaded down with a string of sausage
That would have split open had it been bigger,
He appeared washed and reverent,
His jauntiness surprising all.

XXXVII

He set off on his business with a flourish,
Ambling on the road at an easy pace,
And a smile played upon his lips
As if it were carnival or contraband.
Then, with a voice that shook all present,
He went from door to door on his quest:
'Did anyone here share their sausages with Vidal?'
'Not here!!!' *'Too bad, I'll go share with someone else!'*

XXXVIII

So Vidal passed the hovels one by one
And the string of sausages was still intact,
For no one piped up and said 'yes, me!'
No matter how many he surveyed.
Humiliated they were by the follies of fortune,
As with a teasing voice he repeated:
'Did you share your sausages with Vidal?'
'Not here!!!' *'Too bad, I'll go share with someone else!'*

XXXIX

Vidal died and time moved onward,
Embers that the cold of marble puts out
Amidst the frozen rubble burying
Everything, from Vidal to his solitary house.
Yet this story lives on and will last forever,
It's passed into proverb along the route,
And when the name of Vidal is mentioned,
More than one mouth even now goes mute.

26

'Dear girl, you the most gorgeous
That sunlight has ever illuminated;
You the star of sweet morning
That in pure inks is basking;
You the flower of flowering peaks,
You the nymph of fresh waters,
You like petal of the lily,
White, pure and mournful.
Who are you, nameless destiny
With such sleepy glances,
With such golden smile,
With features so candid?
Perhaps you were born of woman
Being so unsullied and well bred?
Perhaps from late breezes,
Perhaps from curtains of mist…
From the tiny bubbles of a river,
From a white cloud perhaps?
Or the foam of ocean
Joined to a sunbeam
Propelled you to appear at dawn
In a wee shell of nacre?
But wherever you come from,
Saddest passion-flower,
For you I feel a pure love
That slowly slays me.
For you night and day,
Like a vague enchanted shadow,
I sigh close to where you live,
Sigh in the winds that blow
Making sounds reverberate
Just like harp-strings

Which with trembling echoes
Tell you of my love.
But say, why are you silent?
Is it because you're alone,
Is it because you live in the peaks
With the songbirds that sing,
While you weep and weep,
Seated under an elm
All dressed in mourning,
All covered in tears.'

'Let me live in the mountains,
Let me be alone,
Let me live with the songbirds
That chirp around me.
Let me dress in mourning,
Drenched in sad teardrops,
Not listening to men's echoes,
Nor to the sound of melodious harps,
For those sounds of love for life
Tear my insides apart,
I hope you, my gallant, by some luck
Can feel that they console you
For an ache that has no cure,
For a misfortune that never ends.
If to their sonorous vibration
The tombstones could only rise up
And the dust that lives in them
Come back to life as if stirred!...
But, quiet, my gallant; don't pluck
The suave harp-strings
That can't give life to those who die,
Nor lift sad tombstones.
Quiet, my gallant, with those songs
That you sing with loving passion,
My lovers are dead

And await me there in the tomb.
For me luck has died,
Hope too has died,
Covered all it had with sadness
And the earth with rank weeds.
Let me live in the mountains,
Let me be solitary,
Let me wear mourning clothes,
Smirched by bitter tears.
For the turtle-dove widowed
Has sworn never to marry,
Nor rest on a green branch,
Nor drink fresh water.'

27

I

What's up with the boyfriend?
Hey! What's with him?
He gives me a look as cold as winter,
Then, at the sewing bee later, he comes and grins!
He wants me to dance with him in the mill yard
And go out on the town, need I say any more?...
What's up with the boyfriend?
So what's with him?

At times, like a guide dog,
Wherever I'm going he comes and follows,
There's no place where I don't run into
Brian with plums and carrying his clogs.
Oh, what a suitor...
Oh, what a guy!

The next moment, what a show-off!
He lets loose yodels all over the place.
Trill!! He's hamming it up so proudly,
Impressing the guys with his prowess.
Boyfriend, are you crazy?
Oh! And if you were?

I can't understand, my love,
How you're carried off by the breezes,
Nor do I get what you're thinking
When it comes to being in love.
Oh, God save me
From you, good Brian!

In my mind I compare you
To martial March with its blizzards:
In the morning, it caresses like roses;
In the evening, it bites like a dog.
What a bad couple
We make! Ow!

II

What's that witch saying,
What'd that betrayer say?
You shroud your heart in mourning
At the bleak insults only a cheater could let fly,
Why do you live suffering for her?
Why if you're in love, do you sob in grief?
Oh yes, she's pretty,
But she betrays.

She dismisses me, saying that who knows
What winds are blowing me around...
Just look what your eyes say, girlfriend,
They lure me one moment, then blow me away.
Even if you're pretty,
You betray.

If sometimes I lovingly call you
And if other times I deny you... wicked girl!
What kind of waters lie quiet
If the wind that rules them stirs up their waves!
And you well know
That you stir things up.

I'm just like a guide dog to the blind in loving you…
As if unlimited love deserves mockery
And with my clogs in my hand or without them
I've trooped after you to the gates of hell.
    I'm just that crazy
And you that much fun.

    So I look to you like a March blizzard!…
Maybe I'm one, but you, precious girlfriend,
You're like March lightning,
That lights the world up, then plunges it into dark.
    We're equals,
    Pretty girl.

28

Castilians of Castile,
You're so good to the Galicians,
When they go to you, they go as roses,
When they come back, they come as slaves.

When he went, he went laughing,
When he came back, he came dying.
The sweet light of my eyes,
The sweet love of my heart.

That man whiter than the snow,
That man full of tenderness,
That one for whom I lived,
Without him living's not for me.

He went to Castile to earn his bread
And rank grain they gave him;
For drink they gave him bile
And sweet grief to nourish him.

They gave him, in short, bitterness
Enough to last a lifetime...
Castilians, Castilians,
You have hearts of iron!

Oh, my dear aching heart
No happiness can now fill,
For it is full of wounded pain
And shrouded in grief.

He died, the one I loved truly,
For me there's no consolation:
All there is for me, Castile,
Is the lousy cash you sent me.

May God permit, Castilians,
Castilians whom I detest,
Better that Galicians die
Than ask for your sustenance.

For you have such vile hearts,
Dry children of the desert,
The bread they earn from you is bitter
And you give it dipped in venom.

There they go, unlucky, fated,
All of them so full of hope
And they come back, oh, empty-handed,
On a deep river of contempt!

They leave poor and come back poor,
Leave robust and come back broken,
Even though they are like roses,
You treat them like slaves.

Castilians of Castile,
You have hearts of steel,
Souls as hard as stone
And no guts inside you!

On thrones of straw you sit,
Without foundation, haughty,
You think our beloved children
Were born to serve you.

And never was such a nasty idea,
Such a criminal thought,
Couched in more fatuous heads
Or in more fatuous feelings.

Castile and Castilians,
All gathered together,
Aren't worth a single blade of grass
From our fresh Galician fields.

Only fetid puddles
Lying on the scorched earth
You have, Castile, to moisten
Those dry lips of yours.

The sea left you forgotten
And far from you its waters flow,
The smooth waves that carry
A hundred plant seeds.

Nor do trees give you shade,
Nor is there shade to catch your breath…
Flatlands and flatlands forever,
Desert and desert forever…

This is exactly, lucky Castile,
What the universe has given you,
Miserable boaster!…
A sad heritage for sure.

In truth, Castile, there's
Nothing as ugly as you are,
You might even say that hell
Is better than Castile.

Why did you have to go, my treasure?
You should never have done it!
Trade little fields in full flower
For huge sad fields without water!

Trade such clear spring waters,
Such rivers that murmur aloud,
For dust so dry that even
The tears of heaven won't moisten.

But oh, you left my side
Without feeling the pain that I did
And over there they took your life,
Over there death was what they gave you.

You died, my cherished one,
And for me there's no consolation,
For where once I saw you, now
I only see a grave.

Sad as night can be,
Heart full of aching,
I beg of God to kill me,
For I no longer want to live.

But since he does not kill me,
I detest Castilians
And must, to your shame,
Keep sighing this chorus:

Castilians of Castile,
You're so good to the Galicians,
When they go to you, they go as roses,
When they come back, they come as slaves.

THE GALICIAN BAGPIPE

[Poem by Ventura Ruiz Aguilera]

To my dear friend Manuel Murguía

I

When the Galician bagpipe
Is played by the poor piper,
I don't know what comes over me,
My eyes sprout tears.
I imagine I see Galicia,
Beautiful, pensive and alone,
Like a woman without her lover,
Like a queen without a crown.
And while the glad beat intones
And the wild throng dances,
The voice of the grave instrument
Sounds so melancholy to me:
To my soul it reveals legions of
Misfortunes, deep grievings,
So I don't know how to tell you
If it sings or it cries.

II

I remember those skies
And those gentle dawns
And those small green fields
And the coo of turtle-doves
And those lakes and mountains
That reach to touch heaven,
All full of perfumes,
Dressed in flowers all,
Where God opens his hand
And sprinkles his treasures:

But oh, how I remember too
That there are those bent down
In the midst of the abundance,
Hunger twists their faces,
So I'm not sure I can tell you
If it sings or it cries.

III

In dreams my spirit meets them
Pure, laughing and pretty,
The shades of the hundred ports
Which grace Galician shores.
And slowly passing,
Like floating cities,
Its hundred proud ships bob
To the raucous sound of waves;
But oh, how I see in them,
Along the gold of its coastlines,
Its tender children dispossessed
Who gaze sadly on Europe,
Begging their bitter bread
From far-off America,
So I'm not sure I can tell you
If it sings or it cries.

IV

Poor Galicia! Your children
Flee or are stolen from you,
Filling with deep grief
Your loving womb.
And like damned pariahs
And like the tribes of Helots

Who bear on their faces
The seal of infamy or dishonour,
Oh, the state forgets them,
The state abandons them
And poverty and death
Rule in their deserted homes.
That's why, when in celebration
The Galician bagpipe is heard,
I'm not sure I can tell you
If it sings or it cries.

V

Hope, Galicia, hope!
Withstand the cross that burdens you,
As blood and tears irrigate
Your dolorous way.
You'll thirst! Honey and vinegar
They'll pass you in abundance
And with crown of thorns
And reed sceptre they'll mock you;
But the time is coming
And when your hour sounds,
You'll rise great and joyful
To the heights of glory.
Today if the Galician bagpipe
Is played by the poor piper,
I'm not sure I can tell you
If it sings or it cries.

29
THE GALICIAN BAGPIPE

[Response by Rosalía de Castro]

To the eminent poet Ventura Ruiz de Aguilera

I

When you intone, poet,
This song on your sighing lyre,
I don't know what comes over me,
But I drown in welling tears,
For before me in my path I see
The virgin martyr you invoke,
Her feet nailed with thorns,
Her hands covered with roses.
In vain the bagpipes playing
A glorious *alborada*
Scatter sounds through the air
That fall in trembling waves.
The wild throng dances to them
In vain in the threshing yard
And such sounds so torment me,
Tell me of things so sad,
That I can tell you:
It doesn't sing, it cries.

II

With you I see those skies,
I see those pale dawns,
I see those flowering fields
Where the doves all coo
And those gigantic mountains
That reach to touch the clouds,

Covered with verdant pine trees
And fragrant flowers.
I see this blessed land
Where God's good overflows
And where handsome angels
Weave brilliant crowns.
But oh, I see also
Haggard shadows passing,
Crickets of iron dragging past
Between mocking smiles,
While the tender bagpipes
Play their glorious *alborada*,
I can tell you:
It doesn't sing, it cries.

III

You speak and my thoughts
See the trembling passage
Of the shades of those hundred ports
That nestle by the waves.
And one by one they're leaving,
Fragile, sad and lonely,
On proud ships that float
Far away on a traitorous sea.
And oh, in them steer
The children of our coastlines
Heading to deplorable America
Where death is handed them with bread,
Dispossessed, asking in vain
For mercy from that country.
While happy the little bagpipe
The poor bagpiper plays,
Yes, I can tell you:
It doesn't sing, it cries.

IV

Poor Galicia, you must never
Call yourself Spanish,
For Spain just forgets you
When you are oh so beautiful!
Even if you were born in disgrace
And she's ashamed of your slowness,
The mother who disdains a child
Can only be called heartless.
No one to help you up
Extends a generous hand;
No one your laments will dry
And humble you cry and cry.
Galicia, you have no state,
You live alone in the world
And your fecund progeny
Scatter in errant hordes,
While sad and solitary,
Spread on the verdant carpet,
You beg hope from the sea,
You implore God for hope.
So even if its notes are festive
And the bagpipe sounds happy,
I can tell you:
It doesn't sing, it cries.

V

'Hope, Galicia, hope!'
How much this cry consoles us!
May God grant it to us, good poet,
But it is a foolish hope.
For before the time arrives
Of such great luck foretold,

Before Galicia rises
Under the cross that weighs it down
On a road so difficult
That it touches the deep abyss,
Perhaps, footworn and thirsty,
It may die of agony.
May God grant, good poet,
Your hope of glory
That from your heart surges,
The virgin martyr crowned,
And this be our recompense
For such deep bitter griefs.
May God grant you this sad tune
That our misery retells,
For only you – among so many! –
Remember our disappointments.
It has the eagerness of a genie,
Soul pure and generous!
And when the Galician bagpipe
You hear off in far Castile
And your heart is asking,
You'll see that it responds
That the sweet Galician bagpipe
Doesn't sing, it cries.

30

I

Come on, little girl,
Come on, wee lass,
Come here and bathe
In the fountain basin.

Come on, Peewee,
Peewee, come here
Or else I'll snag you
With the tooth of the devil.

Look at the clean water!
How lovely and fresh!
Come here and bathe,
It's so lovely, creature.

As God's my witness,
If there'd never been water,
This mortal body
Would turn back into mud.

Kids, come and bathe,
Get over here quickly,
The face to start with
And then wee feet.

Oh, what a sweetie!
What a wonderful girl!
After a bath
You are just like a rose.

And this little sir
That I hold in my lap
After a scrub
Is just like a cabbage.

Oh, cute as a cuckoo!
Oh, what a wee saint!
Come into my arms,
I'll give you a kiss.

Wee eyes so glorious!
Little magical face!
Hug me hard,
Sweet heart of butter!

Run now, run,
So Antonia can comb you,
Run, she'll give you
A mug of milk.

Run now, run
To your daddy, wee Marica,
He's eating onions
With bread and sardine.

II

As God is my witness,
The figs are still hard!
But we'll stuff ourselves
The moment they're ripe!

He and me too
And my friend down below,
We're going to have
To let out our skirts.

Rich tree of figs,
May God bless you,
You've caused me, I swear,
A swollen gut!

Hey, you with the eggs
Heading past on the road,
How many dozens
Did you pluck from the nest?

One, that's all!
Quit pulling my leg!
For a tall tale like that
You should go to confession!

If you give me six eggs,
I'll make you a fry-up,
One even the king
Would envy I'll make.

Since you don't want to,
I hope you get caught
On the road by a whirlwind,
With a sack of spit.

III

Pull, oh, pull, oh,
John, on the burro!
Look, the puppy Pedro
Nips at your heels!

Oh, how sad it is
To see that pup
Leap into the buzz
Of the crazy skirmish!

That devil of a John
Neither runs nor kicks!
Good luck to the one
Who gnaws your bones.

You fat hens! Scram!
You fat little cluckers!
Get outa here,
You're scaring the burros.

Peck, peck,
Sweet dove, peck,
Carry a seed
To your chick in your beak.

Get outa here, dog,
Go bark in the hayloft,
I know that you like
Its devil of a smell!

Get outa here, dog,
Who likes fish so much!
But to your master
You just cost him money.

Shoo! Shoo!
That devil of a cat!
How he gorges himself
Licking sauce off the plate!

You're about to burst,
You greedy roly-poly!
Even in your throat
You've got a lump!

Go butt heads, buckaroo,
With the bobtail cat,
Until you've left him
Without any fur.

As for me, if ever
He crosses my path,
I'll have to give him
A whack on the back.

Tsk, tsk, that one
Who can't follow the Mass,
Nor enter the church,
Nor wear a real shirt!

Oh, that chicken
Jumped over the wall!
I know that it wants
To be eaten right now!

Scram outa here,
You damnable clucker,
Scram outa here,
Don't kill my hens.

Scram outa here,
You thieving clucker,
Scram outa here,
Go home to your master.

31

When moonlight appears
And sun hides in the sea,
All is silence in the fields,
All on the riverbank sleep.
The flatlands are empty,
The peaks without sheep,
The spring without vibrant roses,
The trees without songbirds.
Frightening is the wind that passes
And moves the giant pines
And to the voice that lifts sadly
Another, sadder, answers.
It's the bells that ring out,
Ring the peel of death,
And say to the heart, 'Don't forget
Those ones whose sleep is eternal.'

How sad! How sad is this hour
When the sun hides itself,
When the pale stars
Timidly glitter!
Over the smudged mountains
Thick fogs are cloaked
And the white house he lives in
Swirls in thick shadow.
In vain I peer and peer
As the veils of dark night
Between it and my eyes
Settle down in betrayal.

What are you up to, my treasure?
Tell me where you are, what you do,
For I await you and you never come,
I call you and you do not answer.
Are you dead, my cherished man?
Swallowed up by deep seas?
Did wild waves carry you off
Or are you lost in the mountains?
I keep asking the breezes,
I keep asking the shepherds,
To the green waves I ask
And no one, oh, answers.
The silent breezes stir softly,
The shepherds don't hear me
And the deaf waves broiling
Break on the rocks.

But you did not die, ingrate,
Nor get lost in the mountains;
Perhaps while I was pining
You took pleasure in my grief.
Mercy on me, have mercy!
For this noble heart of mine
Was to you a spindly reed
That the least wind twists.
And in return you forget me!
You give me bile, leave me to death…
This is how, unlucky me,
Men reward those who so love them!
But no matter! I loved you well…
I'll love you always… Thus it is
For the stalwart one who firmly
Gave you her heart and soul.
You have my heart there,
You can kill it easily if you wish,
But as you live in it,
If you kill it, you too die.

32

I

If you'd come to see us, Marica, the other day
At the festival of O Seixo by the sea,
You'd have laughed, Marica, as never before
Under the pines of the green pine grove.

In the shade of the pines, Marica, what foolish
Things took place! What crazy giggling!
Wild up above and wild down below,
We came, went, and the bass drum... boom, boom!

Gentle pinches, happy tumbling,
Shouts, leaps, tales that delight,
All drunken, all so happy...
And our Boss Lady behind the barrel.

II

Unlucky girl! You missed a copious feast!...
You'd have sung, drank, slept and all that,
In a swarm all together with
Young and old folk from every which where.

With blurred sight, with sleepy eyes,
Smiling, feasting, carousing and even more,
What hugs and flirty looks they trade,
Our lively girls with the guys from Cadiz!

Under rich silk umbrellas opened
In circles huge and round,
Everyone tipsy, what things they were saying!
And our Boss Lady behind the barrel.

III

Yes, she who is usually so serious and snobby,
Her ears so fine, her hands so small,
Deaf she'd become and babbling like seven
With poor and rich, with pups and pigs.

Her hubby relaxing at such great largesse,
That in his lady he didn't often see,
As if, my precious, he'd got down from the burro
– Bing, bang! – and bolted upriver at a run.

And the boss lady smiles with eyes half-shut,
Eating chestnuts and honey with wine …
What a feast, Marica!… Everyone half-cut…
And our Boss Lady behind the barrel.

33

How softly it's raining,
How softly it rains;
How softly it's raining,
Over at Laíño
And over at Lestrove.

How the sad white cloud
Troubles the sun's restless light
As it covers and uncovers it,
Passes, turns, spins back and rises,
Laughing white plume.

Later scattered in the distance
By the fleeing breezes,
Distended, shadowed,
In space set loose,
It falls glittering in vibrant rays.

Mysterious waterer,
Fine drizzle settles on the soil
In exquisite undulations,
Drenching, at the riverbank,
Flower after flower, plot after plot.

It seems to be a light gas
That the wind subtly moves,
In floating waves it passes
Refreshing as it embraces
What the ardent sun reveals.

How softly it's raining
On the plains of Campaña!
How it soaks as it passes
The rich grasses of Laíño!
How Ponte is bathed in the sun!

At Caldas all's dark,
Blue sky blazes in Adina,
Transparent, clean and pure;
From Arretén in the harsh peaks
A pilgrim cloud flits by.

Sadly it passes and touches
With feet of white snow,
With a fine cool mouth.
Sadly it passes, invokes heaven
And dares to kiss earth.

Sadly it goes when it abates,
Vaporous, alone and mute,
When it beats its wings softly
Like a heart that throbs
Wounded by a sudden pang.

It's how I imagine the sad shade
Of my mother, wandering alone
In the spheres where she lives;
She resists going to glory
For the sake of those she awaits and loves.

I see the forest in brown shadow,
Its limbs all entangled,
Not for nothing it bears the king's name,
For there the wild wind darkens,
Reddens and explodes with courage.

And Palacio, solemn and grave,
How it basks in pure light!
It seems a laden ship
That cannot return to sea,
Washed up on fresh fenland.

I see Valga at the beautiful edge
Of a path that's all silver,
Like an immaculate virgin,
Sweetly seated on a bed of roses,
Wearing scarlet robes.

I see San Lois shining,
Purely tinted where it basks,
Showing off sun and shadow,
Restfully gazing out at
Mountains, waters and greenery.

And in green branches Padrón,
Pale fairy at the foot of a river,
Fruit in flower that I've desired,
In the distance it's lost to sight
Beneath a blanket of dew.

What a full-blown white sail
Flits alone between the corn-stalks,
Mysterious pure star!
The wind says to it as it blows close:
'Fly, little butterfly, fly!'

The gentle estuary laps
With a gentle murmur,
That's born of forest shade
Beneath an awning of happiness,
In the heat of loving sun.

Sun of Italy, sun of *amore*!...
You light up a better landscape,
Yours is rosier, even greener,
Clearer sky, more suave in colour,
Do you see from the gulf between mists?

Sun of Italy, I don't long
To feel your ardent rays!
I gaze at a more temperate sun,
Here I breathe gently
In a lasting eternal May.

In this land such enchantment
Breathes... Poor or sad,
Rich or full till bursting,
It caresses all
Who beneath its skies are found!

Those who are born there,
Those whom Galicia cherishes,
Away they are saddened,
For they leave wounded by love
Of the one who nursed them.

The mother pines for her children.
Deaf, sad, plaintive, she
Sobs, cries and sighs
And does not stop until she sees them
Arrived safely, every last one.

Poor mother, how much I love you!
Mother of my mother too!
I prefer your loving soil
To whatever is grand or awe-inspiring
On all the earth put together.

How can I not if I now alight
In a landscape of silver and roses,
Where life is so deeply cherished
As my eyes brim with
Sweet loving memories.

Woods, house, tombs,
Bell towers and bells
With slow gentle sounds
That awaken, oh, tenderness
That will never be in vain!

They were the bells that rang out
When my babes were born there;
They were those that wept,
They were those that tolled,
When my grandparents died.

They were those that gaily
Rang to beckon me gently
In the gold of early morning,
Away from my mother, with poetry
And kisses all at once.

I still see where I played
With the girls whom I loved,
The wee yard where I played,
The rose bushes I cared for
And the fountain where I drank.

I see the solitary street
A serene sun bathes in peace,
With no contrary hand to trouble it,
Always the same, it never changes,
Flat prairie to amenable fields.

And I also see now in mourning
The noble house of Arretén
Where my mother was born,
It's now like an abandoned widow
That slumps sad beneath an oak.

There it is, a shade that's lost,
A soundless voice, body without soul,
Amazon sorely wounded
Who in realizing she is dying
Drifts to sleep in deafening calm.

Casa grande they once called it
In another luckier time
When the poor implored it
And, sated, warmed themselves
At its loving fire.

Casa grande when a saintly
Venerable gentleman[2]
With peaceful noble charm
Under the folds of his cloak
Sheltered those who begged.

When the hymns in the chapel
Of the *Gran casa* resound
With fervour and simple faith,
Rich fruit of the seed
That the worthy men had sown.

---

[2] The truly evangelical virtues of this gentleman, so beloved by those who knew him, inspired me to write a book, which I'll soon publish as *My Grandfather's Story*. In it, I pay a tribute of admiration and love to a man whose great wisdom consisted in always blindly doing good, with an affectionate hand.

Now everything gone silent
Causes fear and dread there,
A frightening spirit lives
In the salons where repose
Has made a nest with sadness.

Laughs, songs, harmony,
Soft music, contentment,
Parties, dances, merriment,
Turned into the sad and cold,
Deaf voice of brute wind.

On the huge patio weeds grow
Vigorous and untamed
And the blackberries that flower
Once held out their fruit,
Ripe, to the children.

And before the deafening silence
No one now comes to alter,
Before the 'I'm gone!' so rude,
A noble crest is seen intact
To counteract the wistful 'I'm no more.'

Strong beams look smug
In their haughty airy shell…
But behind the vain 'I am'
Poor human pride is visible,
Humbled and dusty.

Behind the dense foliage
There are aching eyes
That watch us, you might say,
And tell us all is a chimera
In this world of sorrows.

Casa grande! Sad house!
That from here I see so alone,
Dark, gloomy, sad mass,
Casa grande! Pass, pass…
You're no more now than a sigh.

With my grandparents now dead
The others have abandoned you,
Your glow has perished
And those who most loved you
Have long left you too.

Month after month, stone after stone,
You go on decaying,
Cinched by ribbons of ivy,
While other plants grow wild,
That's how the world goes round.

But what light, what colours,
In the spaces open up!
The fading sun glows
And the rainbow just born
Unleashes its long ribbon.

How softly it's raining,
How softly it rains;
How softly it's raining,
Over at Laíño
And over at Lestrove.

34

My dear wondrous Margaret,
To whom can I compare you?
I've never seen another like you
On land or on sea.

There is, wondrous one
So pretty and so precious,
No star that shines like you,
Nor rose that opens.

No radiance, no diamond,
No transparent moon,
Gives off more loving light
Than does your shining face.

Not even the cling-peach flower
Or the purple-tinged rose,
Nor the snows on the mountains,
Nor the brilliance of the dawn.

No gay sun all golden,
Nor stream of pure water,
My wonderful Margaret,
Can match you for beauty.

To whom can I compare you,
My dear wondrous Margaret,
When you are the angel of love
Elected by the angels?

Only the Virgin is more beautiful
Than thou were, wondrous one,
And your face as it moves
Banishes the menacing devil.

I live in love with you
And think of you with fervour
And I know it would please you,
This pure and wondrous love.

Would that I could, oh, that I could,
Live safely at your side,
Spring that pours out honey,
Pure font of tenderness!

At your side, far from the world,
I feel so happily protected
That never for vain pleasure
Would I turn my gaze away.

On the mountain where you live,
There's such good air to breathe,
Whatever runs most from the world
Only there can sigh relief.

My wonderful Margaret,
My Margaret so wondrous,
You have a house in the mountains,
Where the songbird sings.

35
ALBORADA[3]

I

Go now dark-
ness – Go get go-
ing – Come on sun-
rise – Keep on open-
ing – Your face whose sm-
ile – Scares off shadows!!!

Sing!...
Songbird sing-
ing – From branch to branch-
ing – So that sun may be ris-
ing – Over verdant moun-
tains – Over peaks so ver-
dant – Delighting grass-
blades – Delighting spring-
waters!...

Sing, delightful songbird,
Sing!
Sing so corn will grow.
Sing!
Sing so light will listen to you.
Sing!
Sing that night has fled.

---

[3] What I found hardest in writing this *alborada* was my wish that it emerge
with a musical flow. I managed this, but at the cost of poetry. It could not have
been done in any other way; the music moves with such a strange air that it is
hard to put any words to it at all.

Dark night
Comes then
And lingers long
With its mantle
Of sadness,
With spells
And frights,
Prophet
Of sorrows,
Sanctuary
Of mourning,
Shelter
Of regrets,
Protector
Of all misfortune,
Leave!...

So that sweet sunrise
May colour the sky
And the trees
It swoons to love
With a semblance
Of gold and silver
Dipped softly
In scarlet.
With robes
Of diamond
It embroiders
The loving sun
Between waves
Of crystal.

Leave!...
Mistress of all misfortune,
For the sun
Shines already

On the beach shells,
For the light
Of day
Dresses the earth in delight,
For the sun
Melts cold frost with love.

II

    Pale sun-
rise – Now arriv-
ing – And in door-
ways – Enters call-
ing – The yet-sleep-
ing – Now await-
ing – Your splendour!…

    Tint…
Of gorgeous dawn
Extends
Caressing
Into windows,
Where the sun
Hovers also,
While far out
At sea it stretches
And flares up in
Living fire,
Then rises,
Fugitive,
Sad wandering
Splendour.

Cantor
Of breezes,
Delightful songbird,
Sing,
Sing so corn will grow.
Cantor
Of sunrise,
Delightful lover,
To the young girls it says
The golden sun is out.

For the piper,
Washed freshly,
Well dressed,
Combed neatly,
Along with
His bagpipe
Is at the door!...
Wow!...

If in saying
What it says to you
It resounds,
It resounds
In a sunrise
So beloved
By young girls
Wild for singing,
Wild for dancing,
So lively they are;
And by old crones
So delighted,
Who make
Merriment reign.

Up, up!
All you girls in the village!
For the sun
And sunrise are here to wake you:
Up, up!
Get up, you crazy youngsters!
Let's whoop it
Up – And yodel 'oh! la! la!!!'…

36

I sing out, I sing, I sang,
It wasn't very graceful,
For never (and I regret it)
Was I a graceful child.
I sang even if badly,
Giving it a whirl,
As do those who can't pull off
Anything the first time.
But onward and slowly,
Getting louder as I went,
I belted out my songs
Without a care in the world.
I would have truly liked
Them to have been prettier;
I would have liked that in them
The sun danced with butterflies,
Quiet water with light
And soft breezes with roses.
That in them are clearly seen
The spume of green waves,
Pale stars of the sky,
Gorgeous plants of earth,
The fogs of sombre shades
That roll in over the mountains;
The cries of the sad owl,
The wee bells that toll,
Spring that laughs
And songbirds that soar.
Sing out and keep singing while
Broken hearts weep.
This and even more I'd like
To have said with graceful tongue;

But where grace fails me
Feelings overwhelm me,
Though they're never enough
To express certain things,
For at times we sing outside
While inside we weep.
It's hard to express what I want,
For I'm not big on expression;
If grace in singing I can't have,
Love of my country overflows me.
I sing out, I sing, I sang,
It wasn't very graceful,
But what else can I do, unlucky me,
If I wasn't born graceful!

APPENDIX: Two Poems Added to the 1909 Edition

These two poems were added to the third, posthumous edition of *Galician Songs* in 1909. They don't belong at the end, to my mind, for poem 36 does close out the book: the woman who was asked to sing in poem 1 is singing regardless of the inadequacy she feels. And yet they complement each other and have their place. One reveals the wiles of women in trying to maintain the economy of the household by conniving to avoid another pregnancy (and her husband's peevish response) and the other articulates the wiles of men who, in old age, are given to drink.

37

Saturday night
Marica dresses the distaff.

'My woman, dress that distaff
And beg off going to Mass,
Pretend you've no blouse to wear
And are threading a spindle.'
'Monday's All Souls, my man,
Let me keep the day;
If I spin thread instead, what'll
My dear Father say in heaven?
Then... Tuesday's Saint Anthony's
And I shouldn't work either,
So the saint will free me
From the lure of the devil.
Wednesday... I won't say!
The husband of Our Lady,
Saint Joseph... if I spin then
They won't take me in heaven.
And Thursday! No need to explain:
The Most Holy Sacrament!
In all seriousness
That day I must keep holy.
And Friday! Memory
Of the Agony of Christ?
I'll spend it beneath the Cross,
My mind on the Holy Passion.
And you, blessed
Saturday of the Holy Virgin,
Whoever breaks your feast day
Must be excommunicated.
But from twelve to one at night

Between Saturday and Sunday
Bring that distaff here, Dominic,
For there's no sin in it.
If you could see how the dew
Pierces me between my rags!
I wrap these rags around me,
For I shiver with cold.'
'I see no rags or canvas
You can use to cover up,
Move closer to the fireplace
Or sit close to the embers.'
'Maybe I'll warm up…
Brrr! Maybe I'll die!'
'Don't catch cold, my woman,
Or I'll go grab the priest.'
'But I want a blanket,
I feel goose-bumps all over.'
'Well, let the saints cover you,
There's no blanket better.
You rested nights and days
So you could give them kisses,
It's them owe you shelter
In your final moments.'

    That's how Landless John
Spoke with his wife
When all that was left of her
Returned sadly to earth;
And, with a few grasses shielding
Her sad mortal coil,
He said to her (I'm not sure
If crying or singing):
And you, my keeper
Of holy and feast days,
Your body glows now
Between the reeds.'

38

'Buddy, as we get old,
The sun makes us cold,
Every creek to us is a river,
An ox every beetle.
My aching back bugs me,
But God take me
If I don't have a thirst
That's enough to give me asthma!
And well, since we're close
To my house... Old buddy,
Come try my wine
And we'll raise up a glass!'
'You go in first!' 'No!' 'Yes.
You're older.' 'You're lying!'
'Your teeth are a dead giveaway!'
'I've more molars than you.
Then let's go in together
And enough of the you-me-you;
Pour out six measures, Manoela,
We've a thirst to dampen,
Fill the jug from the barrel
And skip the wine from Ulla,
It's only good for raising a ruckus,
Use the one from Ribeiro...
Bottoms up, bottoms up!' 'It does us good,
For without these consolations
We old guys would be wandering
More lonely than the plague.'
'It's a bit sour!' 'What a drag!
Gone sour or not, old buddy,
After God, long live wine!'
'And will there be wine in heaven?

Bottoms up, bottoms up!' 'Good thing!
It goes down like syrup!'
'My buddy, the wise
Need neither wheat nor corn-bread.'
'It's okay when it's warm,
But my wine is better.'
'What, no way!' 'Let's try it, you devil,
Now come to my house.'
'Take it easy, friend.
Mine's fine for the moment!'
'Well, let's fill another glass,
Then come and try mine with me.'
'Good idea. Come on, legs, get up!
Heart, you already beat hotly;
We could do a square dance
With one foot in a sieve.'
'What the devil…
Are we going or not going?
Sometimes we seem to be going,
Then I imagine I've arrived.'
'Drop all that, Frankie,
I'm off like an avalanche
And when the rain stops,
I might hear the cuckoo sing.'
'Never mind that, I do believe
We're almost at my door,
But step carefully, we're going
Through the sheep-pen.'
'You liar… I'm heading straight
For the wine cellar, glutton!'
'But let me go in first,
The dew bothers me.'
'Heavenly Saint Lucy…
Everything looks blurry;
Just between you and me:
Is it night or day?'

'If I knew, I'd have grey hair!
But in secret I tell you,
This blindness, my friend,
Is the fault of the eyelids.
Now sit down and let's drink:
I'm thirsty!… Ah! Whaddya think?'
'If I didn't feel so lousy…'
'Lousy! Strong guys like us?
You greedy-guts… Do
I have to explain?' 'Of course!'
'Drink gets you drunk
And if I may say so… right to Angrois.'
'It's this wine of yours! Hell!
It's drinkable,
But, buddy, if you ask me,
The one I have is better.'
'That's not true!' 'Whaddya mean?
It's time to come with me
And tell me, if you're my friend,
If mine's not much better.'
'Could be!… As for your wine cellar,
Tell me when we get there,
I've got a devil of a thirst…
And that looks like lightning.'
'Hey, buddy boy, that's
Not lightning or thunder;
You've got fire in your eyes
And your throat begs for wine.
Oh! Get your feet moving,
We've reached the spigot,
And drink; as Philippa says,
Thirst makes you queasy.'
'Whoa…! Holy shit, it's strong;
I swigged the whole glass:
You've a wine that I swear
Would awaken the dead.'

'And so? Speak of the devil!
And no word of an Our Father.'
'It's good, but as the saying goes:
Mine's even better!'

     And back and forth on the path
The two buddies drank so much
That they'll never again
Taste water or wine.
With guts round as grapes
After so much sipping,
They dragged them off to the grave
From right under the barrel.

GLOSSARY

At the end of *Galician Songs*, Manuel Murguía, Rosalía de Castro's husband, included a glossary – a list of Galician words used in the text together with Spanish definitions – as a way of explaining Galician words to Spanish readers. In an English translation, there is clearly no need to publish the glossary. Yet the words are so beautiful all on their own and I wanted to include them as a chorus of words in Galician, a chant, a gift, a return.

GLOSSARY (as a chorus of words)

Abó, Abofé, Abofellas, Abondo, Achar, Adoito, Aeito, Afacer, Afacerse,
Agarimo, Agoirar, Aló, Alomear, Alleo, Amoras, Antroido, Antroidada,
Año, Apurrar, Arrepuiñadas, Arrescender, Aturuxar, Aturuxo, Axexar

Bagoas, Balar, Balocas, Bán, Batalada, Bater, Bén, Berce, Berrar, Bica,
Bico, Bicar, Bòla, Boxe, Bran, Brandida, Brañas, Brétema, Bulir

Cachon, Cadela, Cáis, Canas, Candeas, Carabel, Carabela, Caris,
Carrapucheiriña, Cas-qui-tó, Chan, Chao, Cheiro, Cheo, Chiar,
Chuchona, Cirolas, Cobiça, Cóchegas, Cocho, Cofia, Coitelo,
Compango, Compaña, Cor, Cores, Corredoira, Corredeira, Cortello,
Cortelliño, Cortiña, Cos, Cospir, de Cote, Crebar, Crechas, Cribo,
Culler, Cunca, Curruncho, Curtiña, Curuto

Deitar, Demoro, Dengue, Derradeira, Diancre, Dipinicar,
Dou non te dera, Dona

É, Eira, Emboucar, Enfouzar, Ensarrapicada. Enxido, Enxidiño, Erguer,
Esfolar, Espallar, Esquencer, Estricadas

Facer, Falangueiro, Falangueira, Feira, Feita, Feitizo, Fenda, Fero,
Fiadas, Fidalga, *Fito á fito*, Fogáx, Folga, Fricol, Fricolada, Frixolada,
Froita, Frolear, Fungueiro

Gaiteira, Gando, Garular

Hortiña

Iña

Lama, Lansaliño, Laña, Lar, Lariño, Larada, Larpeiro, Liña, Loitar,
Lombo, Lua, Luar, Lurpia

Má, Magoa, Maino, Mainiño, Malpocado, Malpocadiño, Mantelo, Matar, Matachin, Maxesa, Meigallo, Meigo, Millo, Mimosa, Moucho, Mouriña, Moura, Muchada, Muhiño

Nabisa, Nantontre, Nay, Neno, Niño, Noces, Noxo

O, O, Orfo, Oubear

Palomas, Palomiñas, Panos, Parolar, Parromeira, Pau, Peitar, Pelica, Pena, Penedo, Peneira, Peçoñosas, Pia, Pifar, Pito, Pitiño, Pombas, Pónla, Portelo, Posto, Pousar, Praticar, Prctiño, Proya

Quinteiro, Quiño

Rabuñar, Racha, Ramallaxe, Raparigo, Rapas, Raxo, Rebotar, Rebuldeira, Rebulir, Regandixa, Rego, Regato, Reloucar, Remorso, Repantrigado, Repoludo, Resólio, Rifar, Ruada, Rueda, Rula, Runxida, Runxindo, Ruxe-ruxe

Salgado, Salgueiro, Saloucos, Sar, Sarpullente, Sarrapio, Seica, Seixos, Sera, Serán, *Seu facer*, Silveira, Sonsa, Sorsa, Suriña

Ten, Tén, Tirar, Tobo, Tolo, Topar, Torrexas, Toxales, Tremar, Trenco, Troncho

Ucha

Vagoas, Vala, Valo, Valado, Valorento, Ven, Vén, Vila, Vincha, Viradoiro

Xa, Xan, Xeito (*non lle dar xeito*), Xoya

Yalma

Zonchos

58	A portly bagpiper	142	A gaita gallega
165	Alborada	75	Acolá enriba
65	*Bells of Bastabales*	77	*Adios rios, adios fontes*
72	*Blessed Saint Anthony*	83	*Airiños, airiños aires*
175	Buddy, as we get old	165	Alborada
105	*But however much he wished*	115	Aló no currunchiño mais hermoso
108	Castilian lady of Castile	27	*As de cantar*
135	*Castilians of Castile*	65	*Campanas de Bastabales*
146	Come on, little girl	151	Cando á lumiña aparece
129	Dear girl, you the most gorgeous	40	*Cantan os galos pr'ó dia*
35	God bless us all, child	108	Castellana de Castilla
77	*Goodbye, rivers, goodbye, springs*	135	*Castellanos de Castilla*
93	*Hey, sweet baby boy, hey*	155	*Como chove mihudiño*
155	*How softly it's raining*	175	Compadre, des qu'un vai vello
80	*I clearly saw the owl there*	35	Dios bendiga todo, nena
64	I loved you so much, girl	60	Dixome nantronte ó Cura
69	I saw you on a clear night	80	*Eu ben vin estar ó moucho*
170	*I sing out, I sing, I sang*	170	*Eu cantar, cantar, cantei*
34	I was born when plants were born	55	Fun un domingo
153	If you'd come to see us,	93	*Hora, meu meniño, hora*
	Marica, the other day	105	*Mais ó que ben quixo un dia*
98	*I'm not saying a thing*	129	Meniña, ti á mais hermosa
83	*Little breezes, breezy breezes*	163	Miña santa Margarida
163	My dear wondrous Margaret	43	*Miña Santiña*
43	*My sweetliness*	34	Nasin cand'as prantas nasen
48	*Our Lady of the Barque*	98	*Non che digo nada*
115	Out in the most lovely spot	48	*Nosa Señora da Barca*
75	Over there atop	91	Pasa rio, pasa rio
91	Roll on, river, roll on, river	132	*¿Qué ten ó mozo?*
40	*Roosters sing the dawn of day*	111	Queridiña d'os meus ollos
87	Ruddy as the golden sun	64	Quixente tanto, meniña
173	*Saturday night*	87	Roxiña cál sol dourado
27	*Sing out, girl*	173	*Sábado á noite*
111	Sweet light of my eyes	72	*San Antonio bendito*
142	The Galician Bagpipe	153	Si á vernos, Marica,
60	The priest once warned me		nantronte viñeras
55	'Twas on a Sunday	58	Un repoludo gaiteiro
132	What's up with the boyfriend?	146	Vente, rapasa
151	When moonlight appears	69	Vint'unha crara noite

1. Lois Pereiro,
Collected Poems

2. Álvaro Cunqueiro,
Folks From Here and There

3. Celso Emilio Ferreiro,
Long Night of Stone

4. Rosalía de Castro,
Galician Songs

Erín Moure
is an award-winning Canadian poet and translator. She has won the Governor
General's Award for poetry, twice been awarded the A. M. Klein Prize for
Poetry and also been nominated for the Griffin Poetry Prize for her work
as a poet and translator. She translates from French, Galician, Portuguese
and Spanish into English, including work by Nicole Brossard, Louise Dupré,
Fernando Pessoa and Andrés Ajens. Her translations of work by the Galician
poet Chus Pato are published by Shearsman Books in the UK/US and by
BuschekBooks in Canada. She currently lives in Montreal, where she
works as a translator and editor.

CPSIA information can be obtained
at www.ICGtesting.com
Printed in the USA
LVHW091523290720
661859LV00004B/445